Charles Eames

RAY EAMES.

Gloria Koenig

CHARLES & RAY EAMES

1907–1978, 1912–1988

Pioneers of Mid-Century Modernism

TASCHEN

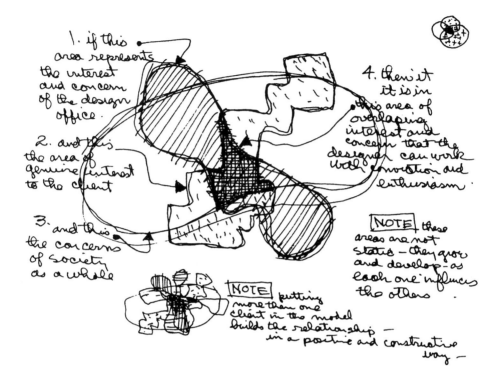

Editor ▶ Peter Gössel, Bremen
Layout ▶ Gössel und Partner, Bremen
Project Manager ▶ Katrin Schumann, Bremen
Copy editor ▶ Christiane Blass, Cologne

Printed in Germany
ISBN 978-3-8228-3651-4

To stay informed about upcoming TASCHEN
titles, please request our magazine at
www.taschen.com/magazine or write to
TASCHEN America, 6671 Sunset Boulevard,
Suite 1508, USA-Los Angeles, CA 90028,
contact-us@taschen.com, Fax: +1-323-463.4442.
We will be happy to send you a free copy of our
magazine which is filled with information about
all of our books.

Illustration page 2 ▶ Self-portrait of Ray and
Charles in the living room of the Eames House,
Pacific Palisades
Above ▶ Charles Eames' conceptual diagram
of the design process, displayed at the 1969
exhibition "What Is Design?" at the Musée des
Arts décoratifs in Paris

Only authentic Eames Furniture gives you the design experience Charles and Ray Eames intended.
Eames furniture is still made today under license
from the Eames Office, LLC which is run by the
Eames family in accordance with Charles and Ray's
intent. Herman Miller, Inc is the sole manufacturer
of Eames furniture in the United States, Asia and
most of the world. Vitra International is the sole
licensee in Europe and the Middle East.

Contents

Introduction

Eames & Walsh Architects, The Meyer House, Huntleigh Village, Missouri, c. 1936–1938

Together they dared to disturb the universe, altering it forever with their Eamesian touch. Flashing across the timeline of the 20th century the husband-and-wife team of Charles and Ray Eames embarked on an astoundingly wide range of enterprises. Through the prism of their office at 901 Washington Boulevard (Venice, California) they projected their singular vision of how the world works and how design can enhance the lives of the people who live in it. They fractured and refracted whatever caught their interest, gaining insight as they assiduously followed the path of the chosen subject of their intellectual focus to its logical conclusion. This was a methodology that worked with everything they touched, be it the Case Study Houses, their hundred or so films, including the classic *Powers of Ten*, the series of exhibitions presented all over the world, or, most famously, their furniture. The primary strategy of the Eames Office in Charles' words was to "bring the most of the best to the greatest number of people for the least." Over the years they did just that, leaving as a legacy the indelible imprint of their distinctive design.

"Although a number of substantial figures in the world of design emerged in the decade following the Festival of Britain, none has made so great an impact on the world, both by his products and his personality, as Charles Eames. It was generally recognized that the *Eames Chair* constituted the first major development in chair design since the Breuer chairs of 1928. After this there followed, in a bewildering succession, toys, films, scientifc researches, lecture tours, special exhibits, three further generations of chairs ... and a great number of awards and citations." This observation by British architectural historian Reyner Banham in his 1981 book *Design by Choice* reflects the awe and admiration generated, then and now, in the worlds of art, architecture, and industrial design, by the office of Charles and Ray Eames.

Charles Eames was born in St. Louis, Missouri on June 17, 1907, to a family he later described as "super middle-class respectable." His father, a veteran of the Civil War, worked for the Pinkerton Detective Agency and later as a security guard at the St. Louis Union Railroad Station. His mother performed the traditional duties of a housewife and mother to Charles and his older sister, Adele. When his father died in 1921 the family moved in with relatives, unable to live on the Civil War widow's pension of $30 a month. From the age of ten Charles worked to help support the family, taking jobs in a printing shop, a grocery store, and a drugstore. By the time he was fourteen he was attending Yeatman High School and working at the Laclede Steel Company as a part-time laborer. There he learned about drawing, engineering, and architecture and first entertained the idea of becoming an architect. In high school he was the poster boy for future success—captain of the football team, a track star, president of his senior class, voted most likely to succeed, and chosen to deliver the valedictory address for his graduating class. In the 1925 high school yearbook he was presciently described as "a man with ideals, courage to stand up for them and ability to live up to them."

At Washington University in St. Louis, which he attended on an architectural scholarship, he continued to excel and was elected president of his freshman class.

Facing page:
Charles and Ray on a Triumph motorcycle

7

However he found himself in basic disagreement with the curriculum, which was Beaux-Arts oriented in the tradition of classical architecture and demanded a conformity of its students that Charles found restrictive. He was a free spirit who pursued his own interests, even when they were diametrically opposed to the school's conventional philosophy. He was intrigued by Frank Lloyd Wright and considered his work to be an essential part of any architectural curriculum, but when he persisted in proposing Wright as a subject of study to his professors he ran into a wall of stubborn resistance. He was advised to cease with his advocacy of Wright and when he didn't was summarily dismissed from the University, a move justified in a report with the statement, "His views were too modern."

While still at Washington University Charles met his first wife, Catherine Dewey Woermann, a fellow architectural student who had already obtained her bachelor's degree from Vassar and held the distinction of being the first woman to be accepted to the University's graduate architectural program. She was the daughter of Frederick

Left:
Charles with Eero Saarinen at a Cranbrook Academy party, c. 1940

Below:
Molded plywood pilot seat, 1943

Woermann, a prominent and influential St. Louis civil engineer who had also attended Washington University. On June 7, 1929, Charles and Catherine were married, and immediately embarked on a European honeymoon, provided by Catherine's parents, during which they studied the classical architecture of France, England, and Germany as well as the work of International Style modernists Le Corbusier, Walter Gropius, and Mies van der Rohe.

Once back from Europe the young couple found themselves in the midst of the Depression, and Charles decided that the only way to get work was to open his own architectural office, which he did with partners Charles Gray and later Walter Pauley. The firm took whatever work it could get, including the commission for the Sweetzer House, a red brick structure with white-painted trim that was a modernized version of the American Colonial style; and the restoration of the Pilgrim Congregational Church, where Charles and Catherine had been married, replacing the spire, some doors, stained glass, and lighting fixtures, all of which bore the modernist mark of Charles' sensibility. Two other residences were built by the firm as well. As Charles struggled to make a living his only child, Lucia Dewey Eames, was born in October of 1930. Over the next few years he took whatever work he could find to make ends meet, including the task of measuring buildings for the Works Progress Administration (WPA) that President Franklin Delano Roosevelt founded to help cut unemployment, which was sweeping the country. It was a desperate time in American history and as Charles watched his friends and colleagues drink themselves into oblivion every night he made a desperate decision of his own, ensconcing his wife and child safely with her parents before leaving, with 75 cents in his pocket, for Mexico.

His 1933 sojourn took him to the Mexican state of San Luis Potosí, the city of Monterrey, and deep into many rural areas, where he traveled and absorbed the culture around him, trading paintings and watercolors for food. It was in Mexico that Charles learned "how very little one needs to survive." The bombardments of heat, sun, dust, and riotous color were primal experiences, visionary concepts that entered his psyche to be stored for future use in the extraordinary body of work that was to come. He returned to St. Louis refreshed, and with his friend Robert Walsh started a new architectural firm, Eames & Walsh, which designed several buildings, including the Dinsmoor House, the Dean House, the Meyer House, and two churches in Arkansas. One of the churches, the Roman Catholic Church of St. Mary in Helena, was published in *Architectural Forum*, and caught the attention of Finnish architect Eliel Saarinen. He was impressed with the traditional building's touches of modernism, such as the unique lighting fixtures leading down the aisle to the altar that depicted the sun, moon, and stars on their spherical globes. Saarinen, who was director of the Cranbrook Academy of Art in Michigan, wrote to the firm at this time and asked about their future projects. When Charles received the commission for the Meyer House, his biggest job to date, he talked it over with Saarinen, traveled to Cranbrook during its construction, and was offered a fellowship to Cranbrook, which he accepted, beginning his first semester in the Architecture and Urban Planning Program in September 1938.

Ray Eames was born Bernice Alexandra Kaiser in Sacramento, California, on December 15, 1912. In spite of her given name, she was called Ray-Ray at home, later just Ray, the name she used throughout her life. Her father, involved in theater work from the time he was a teenager, had been sent to Sacramento to take over management of the Grand Theater. She was raised in a warm and protective environment, perhaps overly so because of the sudden death of her older sister at the age of two. Doted upon, Ray thrived, and when she was only three began to draw, showing an early aptitude as an artist. A few years later she began taking ballet lessons from a local teacher who had been a member of the Russian Ballet, and she has said of that time that "the underlying element ... was the sense of discipline and devotion." At Sacramento High School she excelled in art, joining the art club and, typically, constantly sketching in a series of notebooks. She graduated in February 1931, and attended Sacramento Junior College only long enough to apply to several East Coast schools. She was accepted at the May Friend Bennett School in Millbrook, New York, considered an excellent finishing school, and traveled across the country with her mother to begin classes in September 1931.

In the lush setting of the Hudson River Valley Ray attended classes and completed her two years at the Bennett School, writing that the setting was "all too beautiful!"

A prototype by the Eames Office for the 1948 MoMA show "International Competition for Low-Cost Furniture Design"
The "minimum" chair was an experiment in less is more, using a minimum number of materials to achieve maximum comfort.

Charles and Ray in their Richard Neutra-
designed Strathmore Avenue apartment
in Westwood

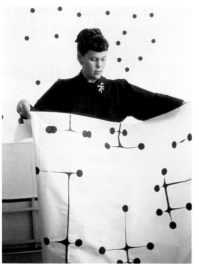

Ray, holding her fabric design *Dot Pattern*
Ray had two award-winning designs at MoMA's
1947 "Competition for Printed Fabrics"

Upon graduating she moved to Manhattan, enrolling in the Art Students League, where the highly respected German émigré painter, Hans Hofmann, was a teacher. When Hofmann opened his own school she and a number of fellow students at the Art Stud ents League went with him. Attending the Hofmann School and working with him ove a period of six years was a pivotal experience in Ray Kaiser's artistic life. Classes in Manhattan by day were enhanced by the culture of the city by night, as the group attended Broadway plays, films, gallery openings, and sampled all the esthetic enter tainment that New York City had to offer. In the summer they drove to Cape Cod, where Hofmann conducted classes in his Provincetown studio. Hofmann was a hard task master, demanding countless drawings and interpretations from his students, but his emphasis on understanding the relationships inherent in structure and color were con cepts that Ray Kaiser was to bring to her work throughout her lifetime.

In 1936 she became a founding member of a somewhat radical group called the American Abstract Artists (AAA), devoting a great deal of her energy and time to meet ings promoting the rights of abstract modernists to have their nonrepresentational work shown in the city's museums and galleries. Ray Kaiser's paintings were exhibited at the first AAA show, at the Manhattan Municipal Art Galleries, and artists such as Lee Krasner, László Moholy-Nagy, and Fernand Léger exhibited their work in the group's subsequent annual shows. In 1939 her mother moved to Florida because of her failing health and Ray joined her there. Ray cared for her mother until her death in 1940, then closed the Florida house, unsure of her plans for the future. At the suggestion of friends she applied to the Cranbrook Academy of Art that summer, and began at tending classes in the Fall semester.

Ray and Charles' stars crossed at Cranbrook, where Charles was the newly appointed head of the Industrial Design Department and Ray a new student interested in al

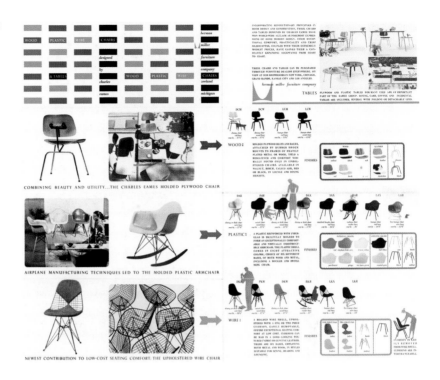

things concerning design. How and where they met can never be known; neither of them revealed the exact circumstances in their lifetime. Charles' grandson, Eames Demetrios, says in his book *An Eames Primer*, "Charles and Ray were two of the most private people imaginable... Unfortunately, this has meant that many of the private events of their life together, such as the precise moment they met and fell in love, were not recorded. But it did happen. It's just that the two people who really knew what happened are gone."

When Charles and Ray began to get to know each other there was a need for discretion as Charles was still married, although, according to Eames Demetrios, "his relationship with Catherine was just about at its breaking point. In fact, they were de facto separated during the summer of 1940." What began as a student-teacher relationship developed into a collaborative team that rocked the world of design and changed it forever.

It is likely that they became acquainted when Ray, who had immediately gravitated to the design and architecture crowd at Cranbrook, pitched in to help prepare the scale models and presentation drawings for a competition that Charles had entered with Eero Saarinen, his friend and colleague at Cranbrook. The 1940 contest "Organic Design in Home Furnishings" was under the auspices of the Museum of Modern Art (MoMA) and in early 1941 it was announced that Charles Eames and Eero Saarinen had won first prize in both the categories they had entered. Prototypes of the scale model furniture were to be made for an exhibition of the "Organic" competition winners scheduled to be held at MoMA that year.

As their attraction deepened Ray, uncomfortable with the clandestine nature of their affair, left Cranbrook after only a few months, going back to New York to stay with friends. Charles asked Catherine for a divorce and in May received the final

Charles and Ray at the Eames Office with staff members Robert Jacobsen, Charles Kratka, Frances Bishop, Don Albinson, Jay Conners, and Fred Usher

papers. On June 20, 1941, Charles Eames and Ray Kaiser were married, and embarked on a life together in California, driving across the country in a new Ford and upon their arrival staying briefly at the Highland Hotel in Hollywood. Within a month or two they began making Los Angeles connections, the most propitious being that with John Entenza, the influential publisher of *Arts & Architecture* magazine. Entenza, who was to become a lifelong friend, introduced the Eameses to Richard Neutra, an Austrian expatriate of growing fame, who offered them a place in his Strathmore Apartments in Westwood.

Charles got a job at MGM Studios, working in the Art Department, which was headed by Cedric Gibbons. Gibbons was married to film star Dolores del Rio and was known for his modernistic "white sets" in the early Fred Astaire-Ginger Rogers films. Charles' skills as a draftsman were put to use drawing architectural renderings of set designs, working with directors Vincente Minelli, George Davis, and Lyle R. Wheeler.

Ray began designing covers for *Arts & Architecture* and both she and Charles contributed articles to it as well. In their spare time in a room in their Strathmore apartment the couple worked on creating the molded plywood furniture that Charles had been engaged with when they met, subjecting it to rigorous tests on a contraption he invented, which they named the "Kazam! machine".

In 1942, with the war in full swing, Charles took a leave of absence from MGM and began working on molded-wood splints for the U.S. Navy. The splints, which were as beautiful as they were practical, were later officially acknowledged for their effectiveness in military action. In their newly formed Plyformed Wood Company, the Eameses manufactured a trial run of 5,000 splints for the Navy, their first experience in mass production. They rented space at 555 Rose Avenue and, anticipating additional military contracts for a plywood litter they were developing as well as other plywood applications, they expanded into larger quarters, at 901 Washington Boulevard in Venice. In

Charles, Ray and John Entenza surveying the Pacific Palisades meadow that Entenza purchased for the Case Study House Program

addition to the financial benefits of their government contracts Charles and Ray had access to the latest technological advances in the materials and machinery being produced during the war years, which they put to good use in the future design and production of their seminal furniture.

Over the next few years the Eameses' friendship with John Entenza flourished as did their involvement with *Arts & Architecture*. The Case Study House Program was officially launched on the magazine's pages in the January 1945 issue. It had its genesis during the war years of 1943 and 1944, when the magazine sponsored a competition called "Design for Postwar Living" which focused on many of the program's underlying principles. In the brave new postwar world where anything seemed possible Entenza commissioned eight architects to build houses that would advocate the principles of modernism while adapting wartime technology to what Ray Eames and Marilyn and John Neuhart in *Eames Design* called "the prefabrication, mass production and industrialization of residential construction." Entenza proposed 34 houses for the program and 23 were actually built. For the Case Study House Program and his own home Entenza purchased a five-acre parcel of land in Pacific Palisades, a pristine meadow o a 150-foot-high bluff overlooking the Pacific Ocean. In this picturesque setting three acres were used for the Entenza House and the Eames House and two acres fo houses by Richard Neutra and Rodney Walker. Between 1945 and 1949 the Eames with Eero Saarinen designed and built Case Study Houses #8 and #9.

Case Study House #8, the Eames House, was designed by and for a professiona couple, to suit their particular lifestyle. It began as an L-shaped design with the studi set against the embankment at the northeast end of the property and a rectilinea "bridge house" extending across the meadow and facing the sea. Later Charles elim inated the "bridge house." The new plans repositioned the house in line with the studi and anchored both in the embankment with a retaining wall. In order to achieve wha

he called "maximum volume from minimum materials," he managed to use the pre fabricated steel sections already delivered to the property to build the new design. green veil of eucalyptus trees screens the house from its neighbor, Case Study Hous #9, as does a man-made mound between them, and provides privacy for both.

Case Study House #9 was designed by Charles Eames and Eero Saarinen for Joh Entenza, a bachelor who wanted an office, a retreat, and a place for entertaining friends Although the plan is based on the same structural system as the Eames House, fou inch steel H-columns and twelve-inch open-web bar joists, it is very different in exe cution, with most of the steel skeleton concealed beneath plaster-covered walls and a interior ceiling of birch wood strips. The 36-foot-long living room with its freestandin fireplace featured windows that opened onto the meadow and a view of the se beyond. Entenza had a small office built, a "womb room" with no windows to distrac him when he wanted to concentrate on work. He sold the house in 1955, and since the

The Aluminum Group designed by Charles Eames for the Herman Miller Furniture Co.

Zeeland, Michigan

This advertisement appears in Fortune Magazine — May 1960

Case Study House #9 has gone through a number of permutations, most of which have obliterated its original design.

Prominently displayed in the living room of the Eames House is the *Eames Lounge Chair and Ottoman*. It is the culmination of years of edgy experimentation, beginning with the furniture Charles designed with Eero Saarinen for the MoMA "Organic Design in Home Furnishings" competition in 1940, continuing across the years in the spare room of Charles and Ray's Strathmore apartment, and finally in that magical arena of design at 901 Washington Boulevard. Here the Eameses developed a lexicon of furniture unlike anything that had gone before, from the 1945 experimental chairs made with new materials developed in the war years to a vast body of work that shaped their future and ours. Together they developed furniture made of plywood, fiberglass, plastic, wire mesh, and aluminum; they invented mass-seating systems for airports, stadiums, schools, and institutions; they made case goods, tables, storage units, and

View of the graphics room at the Eames Office at 901 Washington Boulevard

stacking chairs, contributing to the comfort of the planet with their engineered art. In 1946, having seen the molded plywood furniture at a MoMA exhibition, Herman Miller Furniture Company became the representative for Eames furniture, pronouncing it in its catalog "the most advanced furniture being produced in the world today," and the company continues to market Eames products to this day. Architect Konrad Wachsmann, a friend of Charles and Ray, summed it up: "The Eames chairs have never been out of production. In furniture, the century is his."

Walnut Stools, 1960

"In doing an exhibition, as in 'Mathematica,' one deliberately tries to let the fun out of the bag," Charles Eames said in his outline for the 1961 exhibition at the California Museum of Science and Industry titled "Mathematica: A World of Numbers and Beyond." Charles and Ray often used the phrase "serious fun" and applied the concept to everything they touched, including their mind-altering exhibitions at which they managed to communicate great gobs of information in palatable form. At the New York World's Fair IBM Pavilion a pioneering multiscreen presentation called *Think* examined the futuristic world of computer processing and helped the viewer begin to grasp some of its salient principles. Other exhibitions followed, including "Nehru: His Life and His India," a traveling exhibition commissioned by the Prime Minister's daughter Indira Ghandi; *Glimpses of the USA*, a 1959 multiscreen extravaganza held in Moscow that extolled a day in the life of America as a means of cultural exchange; "Photography & the City" held at the Smithsonian Institution in 1968; "What Is Design?" a composite exhibition of the work of five international architects in which each answered a question about the meaning of design; "A Computer Perspective," which traced the history of the data processor and computer with an explanatory "History Wall;" "Copernicus," celebrating the quincentenary of the astronomer's birth; and in 1975 "The World of Franklin and Jefferson," a traveling exhibition produced in cooperation with the Metropolitan Museum of Art as part of the nation's Bicentennial celebration.

Running like a celluloid thread through all of Charles and Ray's endeavors was a series of short films, begun after the war when experimental cinema was flourishing. "They're not really films," Charles said. "They are just attempts to get across an idea."

This was a manifesto for the Eameses, whose exhibitions, multimedia, multiscreen, and film presentations were all intellectual call-to-arms to reach and educate the viewer. Filtered through their elegant sensibilities, the "information overload" they deliberately sought was sometimes overwhelming but always enlightening, presenting ideas with a bombardment of fast cuts, still images, animation, wild color, and music —which was often provided by Elmer Bernstein, the celebrated Hollywood film composer. From 1950 to 1978 they produced more than a hundred films, from two to 22 minutes long, on subjects ranging from the early *Parade* and *Blacktop*, both of which won awards at the Edinburgh International Film Festival in 1954, to their timeless masterpiece, *Powers of Ten*. Many of the films were sponsored by corporations and the federal government. IBM, having seen the 1953 film *A Communication Primer*, which explained the use of the computer in everyday terms, commissioned Charles and Ray to expand on the theme, which they did in the 1957 *The Information Machine*. All together they created 50 films, books, and exhibitions for IBM. They also produced sponsored films for ABC, CBS, Time Inc., Boeing, and Polaroid, all of them promoting the respective products in unique and innovative ways.

After Charles' death in 1978 Ray spent the rest of her life organizing, cataloging, and writing about their vast output. She died in 1988, ten years to the day after her husband, telling a friend the day before, "I know what day tomorrow is." The archive of words, drawings, and images by Charles and Ray Eames is housed in three Library of Congress divisions, and the Vitra Design Museum in Weil am Rhein, Germany, holds the collection of Eames furniture, prototypes, and experiments. The furniture continues to be manufactured and sold by the Herman Miller Furniture Company, and is also sold by the Vitra Design Museum. Under the supervision of Charles' grandson, Eames Demetrios, the Eames House and Studio is open by appointment to students and scholars from all over the world, as is the Eames Gallery and Store in Santa Monica. In 2004 the Eames Foundation was established to preserve Eames House and the work of Charles and Ray Eames for future generations.

Early molded plywood experimental chair models designed with Eero Saarinen for MoMA's "Organic Design in Home Furnishings" competition in 1940

The competition was called "Organic Design in Home Furnishings," and it was announced in 1940 by the MoMA's director of design, Eliot Noyes. He had organized the contest in response to what he felt was a stagnant state in furniture design. Noyes said in his brief for the contest, "In the field of home furnishings there has been no outstanding design developments in recent years. A new way of living is developing however ... requiring an adequate solution which takes into consideration the present social, economic, technical and aesthetic trends ..." An unusual bonus of the MoMA competition was the pledge by twelve leading department stores to manufacture and market the winning designs. The contest touched a nerve in the world of art and architecture, eliciting 585 entries from across the country, including five from the Cranbrook Academy of Art in Michigan.

One of the Cranbrook entries was from the team of Charles Eames and Eero Saarinen. Together they entered two categories consisting of molded shell chairs, case goods, and tables.

They won first place in the competition in the two categories, submitting photographs of an amazing scale model that was so realistic that the MoMA judges assumed it was of full-scale prototypes. The furniture, including five chairs, two sofas, and a coffee table and end table, was displayed on miniature rugs and draperies created at Cranbrook's weaving department, and Cranbrook students Don Albinson, Harry Bertoia, and Ray Kaiser worked on preparing the models and entry drawings. Eames and Saarinen focused on making a curvilinear chair from a single piece of molded plywood that was comfortable, inexpensive, and could be mass-produced. The MoMA catalog states of the Eames and Saarinen entries, "a significant innovation was that a manufacturing method never previously applied to furniture was employed to make a light structural shell consisting of layers of plastic glue and wood veneers molded in three-dimensional forms." When the time came to market the winning chairs they proved difficult to produce, the structure of their compound curves requiring costly hand finishing. The latest techniques of the auto industry were incorporated in the original design of the seat furniture, using a method of cycle welding and rubber shock mounts developed by Chrysler to attach the chair's aluminum legs to the seat. However, a moratorium on materials was declared because of the impending war and the new innovations in technology were reserved for the military. As a result of these problems the limited production for the MoMA exhibition was prohibitively expensive and it was clear that the idealistic goal of mass production at affordable prices was not yet achievable.

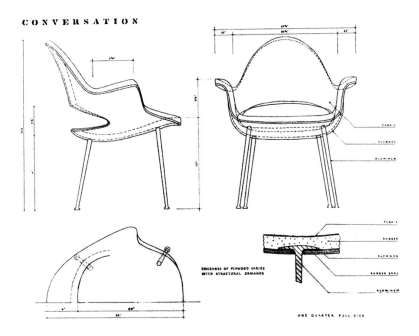

Specification panel for submission to the "Organic Design in Home Furnishings" Competition

1940–1945 ▸ Molded Plywood Productions

plywood sheet for the glider's tail section
being set into a molding machine.

The Kazam! machine

The Kazam! machine must have been a source of laughter, intense labor, frustration, and accomplishment to the young couple in the Strathmore Apartments, who had recently arrived from back east. Charles had smuggled in the necessary parts to build his invention in the spare bedroom—roughly 2 x 4 feet of lumber, electric coils, plaster, and a bicycle pump were all brought into the apartment surreptitiously, most likely by night. The device, named for the magician's saying "Ala Kazam," was designed to mold sheets of plywood into curvilinear furniture, layering the plies with coats of glue and alternating the wood grain for greater strength. The veneers were set into a plaster mold that was wired with electric elements, sheathed with an inflatable balloon-like membrane, and tightly clamped into the apparatus for a period of four to six hours, until the glue had dried. During this time air was pumped into the membrane regularly to keep up the pressure on the drying plywood—hence the bicycle pump, to provide compression. Technology and artistry came together in some of Charles and Ray's experiments with the Kazam! machine, and several wood sculptures they created with it are amazingly beautiful works of art. This ingenious contraption invented by Charles was integral to the future evolution of molded plywood furniture.

At the end of 1941 a physician friend from St. Louis who was stationed in nearby San Diego came to visit the Eameses at their apartment in Westwood. When he saw the Kazam! machine he suggested to Charles and Ray that they adapt their techniques for molding plywood to making wooden splints for the military. He told them that wounded GIs were having problems with the metal splints in current use, which didn't conform to the natural shape of a human limb and as a result often cracked, causing

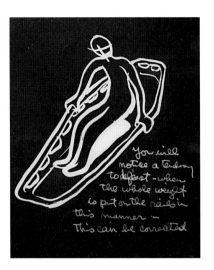

Charles' drawing and explanatory text of the molded plywood body litter prototype, which was never produced

further damage to the leg. Charles and Ray, with their usual innovative gusto, threw themselves into the challenge of designing a functional plywood leg splint, for which Charles subjected himself to the painful process of making a plaster mold of his own leg. Early in 1942, when they had a satisfactory prototype, they drove to San Diego to meet with the U.S. Navy. After being sent back to the drawing board for further revisions, they began mass producing in November 1942 with an order from the Navy for 5,000 splints, which grew to 150,000 by the war's end. With the financial support of John Entenza they opened their first shop, on Santa Monica Boulevard, forming the Plyformed Wood Company, and as Navy orders increased they moved to larger quarters, first to 555 Rose Avenue and then to 901 Washington Boulevard in Venice where the Eameses stayed for the remainder of their careers. Once the production of the leg splints, made of Douglas fir layered with birch or mahogany veneers, was well under way, experiments began for arm splints and a body litter, neither of which was ever produced.

The expanded space at 901 Washington Boulevard was retooled to accommodate the particular specifications of their military orders, and a series of spinoffs of the original Kazam! machine was invented as a result. In addition to the splints, the office worked on developing molded plywood aircraft parts for the aerospace industry. For Vultee Aircraft they worked on vertical and horizontal stabilizers for the Vultee BT15 Trainer as well as other airplane parts, including a molded plywood pilot seat and a plywood gas tank. In 1943 the Eames Office was contacted to produce "blisters," part of the nose section of an experimental glider called the "Flying Flatcar" or CG-16. The cargo glider, to be used for transporting military equipment and large enough to hold two jeeps, incorporated molded plywood parts as substitute for metals the manufacturer couldn't use because of wartime restrictions. Although one prototype was built and tested it was discontinued after an accident that killed the pilot and a passenger.

The military commissions provided invaluable experience as well as access to priority materials to use in the ongoing development of molded plywood furniture which, by 1945, was once more becoming a top priority. "Low-cost high-quality" furniture was the democratic mantra of the Eames Office and their goal was socially conscious standarization and assembly-line production for returning GIs. "The idea was to do a piece of furniture that would be simple and yet comfortable," Charles Eames said of that experimental work. "It would be a chair on which mass production would not have anything but a positive influence; it would have in its appearance the essence of the method that produced it." Staff member Gregory Ain had developed a new wood press with steel parts that increased pressure without splintering the wood plies, and new prototypes with increasingly complex curves resulted. Experiments with seats, backs, and chair legs produced many variations on the central theme, and when the problem of bonding parts and materials together was solved with a "military issue" synthetic glue the possibility of mass-produced chairs became a reality.

Molded plywood sculpture (26 1/2 x 37 3/4 inches) created on the famous Kazam! machine in Charles and Ray's apartment in Westwood

Experimental three-piece molded-plywood lounge chair, 1946

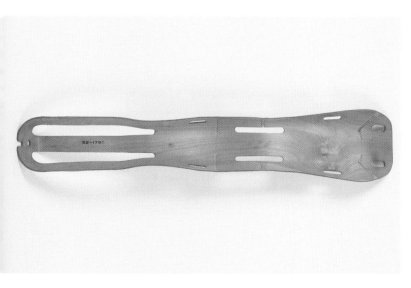

Leg splint

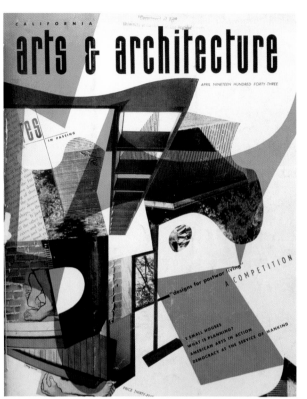

CALIFORNIA

arts & architecture

APRIL NINETEEN HUNDRED FORTY-THREE

"designs for postwar living"

A COMPETITION

2 SMALL HOUSES
WHAT IS PLANNING?
AMERICAN ARTS IN ACTION
DEMOCRACY AT THE SERVICE OF MANKIND

PRICE THIRTY CENTS

CALIFORNIA

arts & architecture

NOVEMBER

1943

CALIFORNIA

arts & architecture

joyeux noël?

stars?

black spot or photo with white

shall it be

it will be december

WHERE

CONTRIBUTORS

and the price 35¢

1943

arts & architecture

1944

JANUARY

PRICE 25 CENTS

1942–1947 ▸ Arts & Architecture Covers

ketches for *Arts & Architecture*

When John Entenza bought what was then known as *California Arts & Architecture* magazine in 1938 his agenda was to bring to the contemporary culture a fresh and innovative view of the arts, and by the time he sold it, in 1962, he had successfully accomplished his goal. Within its covers luminaries such as Dalton Trumbo, Rudolf Michael Schindler, Jackson Pollock, and Richard Buckminster Fuller were given a forum for their avant-garde and often radical views, and the covers themselves were powerful emissaries of the magazine's contents. Los Angeles graphic designer Alvin Lustig designed the title typography as well as several covers, and other cover artists included Herbert Matter, Fred Usher, and Ray Eames.

"Whatever Ray touched turned to beauty," Joseph Giovannini said of his friend Ray Eames, "... whether a table setting of Chinese bowls, a tiny bouqet of violets wrapped in foil, or an arrangement of objects on a shelf." This ineffable quality permeated all the covers she produced for *Arts & Architecture* magazine from 1942 to 1947, and collectively they exemplify the magazine's underlying egalitarian philosophy. Her signature style managed to convey the message of each issue's contents, letting the reader know what was inside before they began to turn the pages. She often used Charles' current photographs in her compositions and also incorporated, if it was relevant, the experimental work going on in the Eames Office at the time.

The series of covers that Ray created for the magazine were powerful representations of its avant-garde modernist philosophy. All of them reflect the influence of her early training in New York with German-born artist and teacher Hans Hofmann, as well as the artists she studied at the time, such as Miró, Picasso, and Calder. She contributed twenty-eight covers in all, from 1942 to 1947.

Facing page:
Arts & Architecture covers

1945–1946 ▸ Plywood Furniture

Eliot Noyes, Director of Industrial Design at MoMA, invited Charles Eames to present his first one-man show at the Museum. It was to be called "New Furniture Designed by Charles Eames" and would feature his ongoing work with molded plywood furniture. Noyes had seen the furniture at the Barclay Hotel in New York, where it was presented at a press preview in December 1945, and again when the New York Architectural League exhibited the show for three weeks in February 1946. An Eames advocate, he wrote an article for *Arts & Architecture* magazine on the plywood furniture, calling it " a compound of aesthetic brilliance and technical inventiveness."

The MoMA show opened on March 13, 1946. The timing was right to bring the new and improved plywood furniture to the public eye, and, it was hoped, into their homes as well. The "new" furniture by the Eames Office had emerged from the crucible of World War II and was designed to fill the needs of the postwar world.

In 1945, with the end of the war in sight and classified information on military technological materials becoming available for domestic use, the Molded Plywood Division of Evans Products, the company formed with Charles in 1942 to manufacture wooden splints for the U.S. Navy, began to make plans for mass production of some of its plywood products. In order to produce high-quality furniture at nominal prices the factory had to be outfitted with the new tooling necessary to utilize the latest industrial technology. The molding techniques of the Kazam! machine had evolved to a level of sophistication that was capable of producing large quantities of furniture efficiently. The five-ply $5/8$-inch-thick chair backs and seats were molded succesfully in ten minutes on the newest Kazam device and the heavier legs took twenty minutes.

When experimentation proved that two-piece chairs were more economical to produce than one-piece models—if one part broke in the mold it could be replaced at far less cost than a whole chair—the factory decided to use separate elements for the chairs, which added a minimalist sleekness to the design. The woods selected for production models were rosewood, walnut, birch, and ash. Chair parts were also available in a variety of coverings, including fabric, Naugahyde and leather. Three of these prototypes, the *Dining Chair Wood* (DCW), the *Lounge Chair Wood* (LCW), and the *Dining Chair Metal* (DCM), were chosen for manufacture because they had the strongest marketing potential, and in winter 1945 the Molded Plywood Division began production. Although the prototypes of the three-legged metal and four-legged wood chairs were on display at the 1946 MoMA show they stopped being produced when they proved to be unstable and were replaced with improved versions.

Also on show was the line of children's furniture produced in 1945 by the Molded Plywood Division of Evans Products, which had manufactured a trial run of 5,000 pieces. The stackable chairs, tables, and matching stools were made of laminated birch and shown in the natural birch or in a range of primary colors. The chairs featured a heart-shaped cutout, promoted as a holding tool for small children, and were designed to be practical in both the home and the classroom setting. Although the trial run was eventually sold to small shops it was not a commercial success in the furniture market

27

A composition in plywood chairs, an ink-on-paper sketch by Ray Eames in the late 1940s

and was eventually discontinued. The children's furniture, the plywood chairs, the upholstered side and lounge chairs, the coffee tables and dining tables, the case goods system, and an early plywood version of the famous *Eames Lounge Chair* constituted the MoMA 1946 show. The installation was designed by the staff of the Eames Office along with the Museum curators, and, as with everything the Eameses did, it was cleverly innovative and well ahead of its time. Panels of graphics, photos, and three-dimensional chair parts designed by Herbert Matter showed viewers how the furniture was made, and high drama was achieved with a noisy tumbling device that demonstrated the structural integrity of a chair by turning it continuously inside a drum filling the exhibition space with the sounds of technology. It was against this exciting and some-what futuristic background that George Nelson, Design Director of the Herman Miller Furniture Company, first introduced Eames furniture to the company's president, D. J. De Pree, resulting in an enduring business relationship that still exists today.

The installation view of the 1946 exhibition "New Furniture Designed by Charles Eames" with a room divider of steel cables that gives the impression of a mirrored wall.

Molded plywood elephant designed as children's furniture and toy, 1945

Plywood chairs with early cycle-welded shock-mount system shown with molded plywood screen

The folding screen, available in 34- or 68-inch heights, was constructed of 9 ¹/₂-inch-wide molded plywood sections with flexible connections that allowed it to be easily adjusted and carried.

Slunk-skin covered *LCW* (*Lounge Chair Wood*)

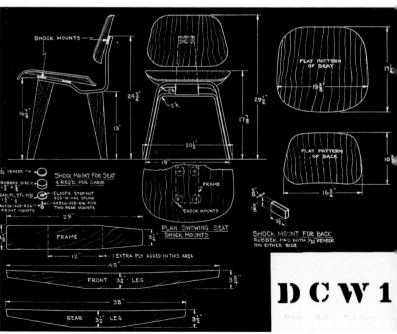

Specifications for the *DCW* (*Dining Chair Wood*)

30

Metal-based molded plywood chairs with screw-attached shock mounts

Folding table with laminated wood top on metal legs

1945–1949·Case Study House #8

203 Chautauqua Boulevard, Pacific Palisades, California

classic vista from the meadow. A green veil
f eucalyptus trees screens the house from its
eighbor, Case Study House #9.

It was Christmas Eve, December 24, 1949, when Charles and Ray Eames finally moved into their new home. Their "dream house" was situated on a promontory 150 feet above the sea and when Ray Eames first saw the site she said "we hocked everything we had to get it." They bought the lot from their friend John Entenza, who had purchased a five-acre parcel in Pacific Palisades from the estate of Will Rogers, with the intent to launch *Arts & Architecture* magazine's ambitious and idealistic Case Study House Program. As Esther McCoy stated in her book *Case Study Houses 1945–1962*, "In 1945 Entenza abandoned his passive role as editor to play a dynamic one in post-war architecture. He announced that the magazine itself had become a client. Eight offices were commissioned to design eight houses ... including Charles Eames and Eero Saarinen." The program was to be an experiment in the social use of technology and the houses would be open to the public for six to eight weeks upon completion. The team of Eames and Saarinen was selected to design Case Study House #8 for the Eameses and Case Study House #9 for John Entenza on three acres of the Pacific Palisades parcel; the other two acres were to be used for Case Study Houses by architect Richard Neutra and designer Rodney Walker.

Ray and Charles had met John Entenza soon after their arrival in Los Angeles in 1941. The Eameses became fast friends with Entenza and by the end of the year Charles was appointed to the board and Ray to the advisory committee of *Arts & Architecture*. By the time the Case Study House Program was announced in 1945 the Eameses were an integral part of the magazine's persona and actively involved in developing the Case Study House Program. The end of World War II was near, and a "guns to plowshares"

cing page:
ont elevation before installation of railroad-
e walkway

Statement of briefs and preliminary designs for Case Study House #8 and Case Study House #9 in the December 1945 issue of *Arts & Architecture*

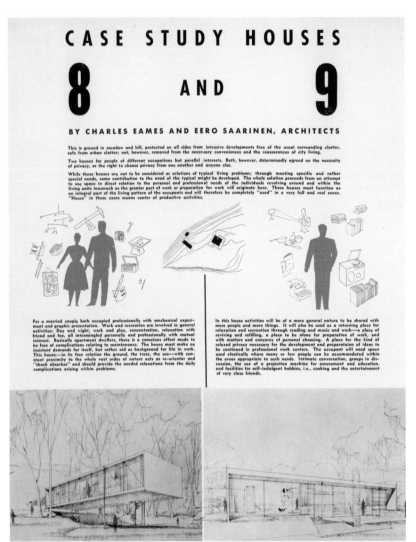

CASE STUDY HOUSES
8 AND 9

BY CHARLES EAMES AND EERO SAARINEN, ARCHITECTS

This is ground in meadow and hill, protected on all sides from intrusive developments free of the usual surrounding clutter, safe from urban clatter; not, however, removed from the necessary conveniences and the reassurances of city living.

Two houses for people of different occupations but parallel interests. Both, however, determinedly agreed on the necessity of privacy, or the right to choose privacy from one another and anyone else.

While these houses are not to be considered as solutions of typical living problems; through meeting specific and rather special needs, some contribution to the need of the typical might be developed. The whole solution proceeds from an attempt to use space in direct relation to the personal and professional needs of the individuals revolving around and within the living units inasmuch as the greater part of work or preparation for work will originate here. These houses must function as an integral part of the living pattern of the occupants and will therefore be completely "used" in a very full and real sense. "House" in these cases means center of productive activities.

For a married couple both occupied professionally with mechanical experiment and graphic presentation. Work and recreation are involved in general activities: Day and night, work and play, concentration, relaxation with friend and foe, all intermingled personally and professionally with mutual interest. Basically apartment dwellers, there is a conscious effort made to be free of complications relating to maintenance. The house must make no insistent demands for itself, but rather aid as background for life in work. This house—in its free relation to the ground, the trees, the sea—with constant proximity to the whole vast order of nature acts as re-orienter and "shock absorber" and should provide the needed relaxations from the daily complications arising within problems.

In this house activities will be of a more general nature to be shared with more people and more things. It will also be used as a returning place for relaxation and recreation through reading and music and work—a place of reviving and refilling, a place to be alone for preparation of work, and with matters and concerns of personal choosing. A place for the kind of relaxed privacy necessary for the development and preparation of ideas to be continued in professional work centers. The occupant will need space used elastically where many or few people can be accommodated within the areas appropriate to such needs. Intimate conversation, groups in discussion, the use of a projection machine for amusement and education, and facilities for self-indulgent hobbies, i.e., cooking and the entertainment of very close friends.

Below:

In this photo, taken by John Entenza, Charles and Ray enjoy the view of the sea from the steel framework of their house, which was assembled in a day and a half.

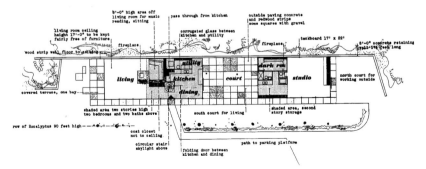

Plan

philosophy of using wartime industrial technology to build homes for returning GIs and alleviate a future housing shortage was an underlying principle of the Program. Projects like Levittown in New York, which mass-produced conventional housing for middle class families, was typical of a growing movement in the country toward providing Americans with affordable housing. It was this perceived need for low-cost single-family homes that the Case Study House Program addressed, using standarized building components to create high-quality modern designs for postwar living.

Case Study Houses #8 and #9 were to share a rolling grassy meadow dotted with eucalyptus trees and rich in wildlife that overlooked the vast expanse of the Pacific Ocean. At night, when the traffic on the Pacific Coast Highway below subsided, the sound of waves crashing filled the darkness. The Eameses and John Entenza loved the meadow and spent much time there before and during construction of their houses,

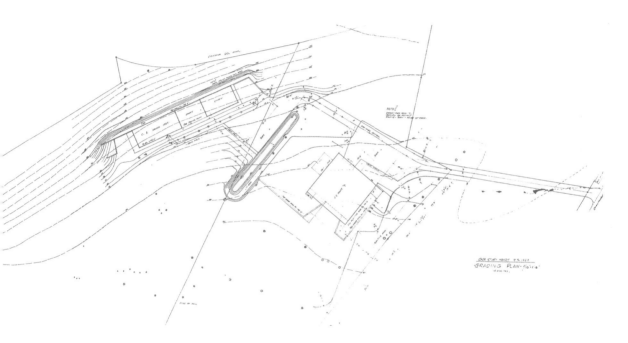

Grading plan

arranging picnics with friends and family, setting up an archery target, flying kites, and enjoying the glorious natural beauty of the setting. The three-acre property was large enough for the two houses to be sited 200 feet apart and allow complete privacy to the owners of each home. In December 1945, the original designs of both houses were published together in an article in *Arts & Architecture*. However, the postwar short-age of industrial materials and the difficulty of obtaining steel for construction delayed completion of the projects several years, Case Study House #8 until 1949 and Case Study House #9 until 1950.

"For a married couple both occupied professionally with mechanical experiment and graphic presentation. ...The house must make no insistent demands for itself, but rather aid as background for life in work. This house—in its free relation to the ground, the trees, the sea—with constant proximity to the whole vast order of nature acts as a re-orienter and shock absorber and should provide the needed relaxations from the daily complications arising within problems." This brief for Case Study House #8, pub-

Unlike the studio, whose upper floor is accessed by a straight staircase, the residential house has a charming spiral staircase.

Facing page:

An ultimate design trinity—the house, the chair, the Eameses

Note ladder hooked across beams, used to change lights and rearrange objects such as the tumbleweed in the upper right corner

lished with its announcement in *Arts & Architecture*, was the template for the singular home that Charles and Ray Eames eventually designed and built for themselves. Their design was the second version of the house, arrived at over the years they spent studying and experiencing the property's landscape as they waited for delivery of construction materials. The original configuration published in 1945 was by the team of Charles Eames and Eero Saarinen, architects, with Edgardo Contini as structural consultant.

These published renderings show separate structures to be built on the property, a residence and an unattached studio, with the studio set against a hillside and the residence swung out from the embankment at a right angle over the meadow. The residence, famously known as the Bridge House, was a rectilinear steel structure elevated from the ground on two steel columns and cantilevered out into space for an unobstructed view of the ocean beyond. The prefabricated parts were ordered but delivery was delayed, and by the time the components arrived on the site in 1948 the Eameses had a completely revised plan in place. Conjecture has it that Charles felt the Bridge House was too similar to a 1934 "sketch for a glass house on a hillside" by Mies van der Rohe that he had seen at a MoMA exhibition in 1947, and both Ray and Charles wanted to preserve the existing eucalyptus trees that were in the path of the Bridge House and keep the structure more integrated with the landscape. As Ray said, "We'd got to love the meadow and the idea of putting a house in the middle of it seemed terrible at that moment. So that's how it happened." The solution was to swing the residence in a 90-degree arc back against the hillside in line with the studio.

Charles did the math and determined how to use the eleven and a half tons of steel that had been ordered for the original design, adapting the precut pieces to the new version. The final plans were published in the May 1949 issue of *Arts & Architecture*. Construction took only a few months once it was under way. A reinforced concrete retaining wall, 175 feet long by 8 feet high, was built along the base of the embankment that bordered the northeast side of the site. The excavated fill was recycled and part of it used as a privacy berm at the property line between the Eames and the Entenza Houses. Like giant pieces of a mammoth erector set the steel sections of the house were assembled to form a structural skeleton in a day and a half. The frame, constructed of 4-inch H-columns and 12-inch open-web joists with an exposed corrugated steel roof decking, was elegantly minimalist in design, which Charles called "thin," and provided interiors of maximum volume that were open and airy.

The architecture projects a lightness of being that historians often compare to traditional Japanese architecture. The 51-foot-long residence has an area of 1,500 square feet and the 37-foot-long studio 1,000 square feet. The two structures and the court between con-sist of seventeen bays, each 7 $^1/_2$ feet wide; eight bays in the living room, five bays in the studio and four bays in the court. To integrate the parts of the whole all the steel sections were painted medium gray, including the facade of the residence. The openings of this neutral background web are filled in with sheet materials of stunning variety of color as well as several variations of glass, transparent, wired and translucent, in the windows and sliding doors. The result is an architectural version of a Mondrian painting framed in nature. Usually attributed to the artistic talents of Ray Eames, this comparison of the front facade to the famous painter, which has often been remarked upon, greatly annoyed her, as Charles' grandson, Eames Demetrios, recalls in his book *An Eames Primer*. Although Ray had met Mondrian in New York and

The Eames House interior was often changed in the 1950s.
This configuration shows tatami mats, a Calder sculpture, and seating facing the living-room patio.

Patio of Eames House
Living room features wooden pilings salvaged from the fire-ravaged pier at Pacific Ocean Park.

was familiar with his style, she pointed out that the facade's effect was "an inevitable result" of the organic design.

Charles' daughter, Lucia Eames Demetrios, uses her personal experience to describe the house's interior: "When one wakes up in the morning, there is the most wonderful shadow play as light filters through the eucalyptus leaves onto the screens and walls. One takes a delighted look at the beautiful pattern of the living room, as seen from above, and then a wonderful spin down the spiral staircase and into the sudden openness of the living room before settling into the kitchen for breakfast." The small seating alcove on the ground floor under the bedroom is a sheltered nook with built-in furniture whereas the main living area soars to a 17-foot-high atrium ceiling. Also on the ground floor is a kitchen, dining alcove, and utility area. A brief written for the living room that specified "pure enjoyment of space in which objects can be placed and taken away" became a lifelong pursuit for Ray and Charles, who used the objects collected from their travels, films, and exhibitions to create an ever-changing spatial collage in their home. Art was assembled, displayed, and constantly rearranged all

through the interior spaces, including the ceiling, where paintings were hung as well as a piece of commemorative tumbleweed collected on their honeymoon trip across the country. A spiral staircase made of steel with treads covered with Charles' beloved plywood leads to the second floor. The bedroom has a sliding door to divide it into two sleeping areas when necessary and two baths complete the upper floor. The studio is also two-storied, and was designed as a studio in which the Eameses could concentrate on films, photographs, models, and other projects, with a darkroom on the first floor, as well as a pullman kitchen, bathroom, a sitting and dining space, and utility area. On the balcony above is a sleeping and storage area. The two structures and the connecting court between established a synergetic background for the Eamses' unique lifestyle.

Panoramic view of the Eames House and studio with courtyard in between showing how the site adapts the architecture seamlessly to nature

Set between the hillside and an existing row of eucalyptus trees, the house draws strength and serenity from both.

ketch of the interior

Case Study House #9 as designed for John Entenza was very different from the Eames House—one is horizontal and one is vertical—yet similar in the structural system and the use of the same industrial materials and methods. The two houses were conceived by the architects to demonstrate the adaptibility of modular steel to the various individual needs of the owners. Entenza's brief states, "In this house activities will be of a more general nature to be shared with more people and more things. It will also be used as a returning place for relaxation and recreation thru reading and music and work—a place of reviving and refilling, a place to be alone for preparation of work, and with matters and concerns of personal choosing." Entenza, who was a bachelor, also mentioned "hobbies, i.e. cooking and the entertainment of very close friends." This description was made manifest in the design elements that endowed the house with a plan specifically geared toward the requirements of the client.

The one-story, 1,600-square-foot Entenza House is a low rectangular box constructed of the same 4-inch H-columns and 12-inch open web bar joists as Case Study House #8, but only four of its twelve supporting steel columns are exposed. The roof is covered with a single flat slab of concrete and the interior ceiling made of birch wood strips. A wall of floor-to-ceiling sliding-glass doors opens the interior of the house to the exterior landscape of the meadow and the ocean beyond. The interior open-plan

acing page:
iving room

41

Sunken area of the living room with built-in furniture

Floor plan

...ayout features a 36-foot-long living room with a decoratively painted freestanding ...replace, a dining room, two bedrooms, two baths, a kitchen, and a study. The study ...vas designed to Entenza's specifications for a completely enclosed, cave-like room ...vith no windows and therefore no distractions from the outside world. Entenza lived ...nd worked in the house for five years before he sold it, and it has since undergone ...nany alterations and modifications to its original design at the hands of its several ...ubsequent owners.

The 36-foot-long living room with window wall looking out onto the meadow and ocean is a metaphor for California indoor-outdoor living. Eames furniture is used including the *DCM* (*Dining Chair Metal*) and the surfboard-like *ETR* (*Elliptical Table Rod Base*).

atio facing the Pacific Ocean

xterior service entrance

acing page:
iew across tree-dotted meadow from Entenza
House patio to Eames House exterior

45

1948 ▸ The Museum of Modern Art
"International Competition for Low-Cost Furniture Design"

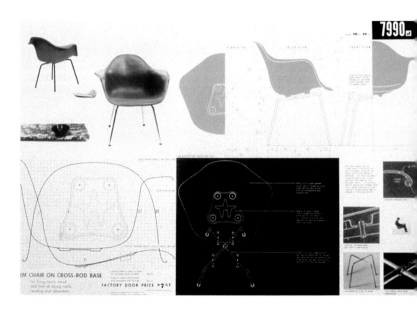

Specification panel of the fiberglass armchair on cross-rod base

In 1948 the Eames Office teamed up with the UCLA School of Engineering to form design and technology team to enter the New York Museum of Modern Art' "International Competition for Low-Cost Furniture Design." Held in response to the perceived postwar need for inexpensive, well-designed furniture for the average famil; the competition was well-received, eliciting 250 entries from the United States an more than 500 entries from European countries. The Museum offered grants c $5,000 each to six chosen design research teams, and the submission in the categor of low-cost seating by the Eames Office with UCLA was a grant recipient. The design were for Eames chairs in a new material, stamped metal, using industrial technology t achieve affordability. "Metal stamping is the technique synonymous with mass prc duction in this country," Charles wrote in the submission text, "yet acceptable furnitur in this material is noticeably absent."

The entry submission was an elegantly contrived package consisting of graphi panels with drawings and captions, specifications, photographs, and text, and was ric in detail, even including a complete breakdown of factory costs, with the manufactu ers' projected profit for two of the prototype chairs. The submission cleverly feature steel and aluminum prototypes of a side chair and an armchair, both with interchange able bases; a "minimum" chair, scaled down to the least common denominator of ma terials that could produce comfort; and a work-in-progress version of an experimenta chair dubbed *La Chaise*, with a proposal panel explaining, "The form of this chair doe not pretend to clearly anticipate the variety of needs it is to fill. These needs are as ye indefinite and the solution of the form is to a large degree intuitive." A photo of Charle and Ray shows them posing on *La Chaise*, with Ray seated in one curve and Charle

La Chaise **proposal panel**
Although *La Chaise* was included in the Museum of Modern Art's permanent collection it was not produced commercially until 1990.

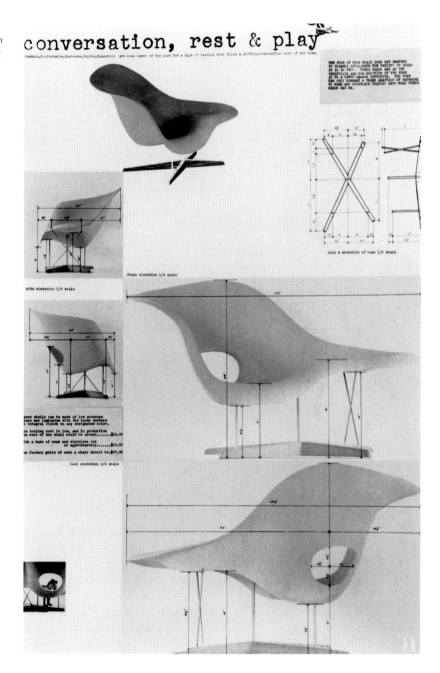

conversation, rest & play

Ray working with staff members on the mold for *La Chaise*
The Eames Office made a full-scale model for the MoMA competition but considered the experimental chair a "work-in-progress."

Production model of *La Chaise* with base of metal bars on oak

sitting comfortably next to her. A jury including department-store magnate Edgar J. Kaufmann, Jr., and famed European architect Ludwig Mies van der Rohe awarded the Eames entry a shared second prize in the Seating Units Category of the competition. An exhibition showcasing the winning entries was scheduled at the Museum for May 1950.

Production of the aluminum and steel prototype chairs for the pending exhibition proved to be more complicated and costly than anticipated. Using an adaptation of the techniques applied in the automobile industry, the chairs' three sections were to be stamped from sheet metal. The plan was to use the hydraulic presses at the UCLA School of Engineering for the metal stamping process, but the presses were rarely available and when scheduling time at the UCLA facility proved too difficult the operation was moved to the Eames Office at 901 Washington Boulevard. Special equipment had to be devised by the staff to simulate the hydraulic press—a block-and-tackle contraption like a drop hammer lifted a 300-pound weight and dropped it repeatedly four feet onto the metal sheet below, which was sandwiched between male/female plaster molds. Although the apparatus had a tendency to break down after a few applications, the office managed to complete three metal-stamped chairs for display at the forthcoming MoMA exhibition. But the process was arduous and Charles began to consider other materials that would be more efficient. The metal armchair, a successor to the 1939 single-shell molded plywood seating Eames and Saarinen developed for the Kleinhans Music Hall, was chosen for an experiment utilizing wartime plastics.

Staff member Don Albinson operating the drop-hammer mold, 1948

Charles and Ray sitting together on *La Chaise*

In late 1949 the Eames Office contacted Zenith Plastics (later Century Plastics) of Gardena, California, to discuss the possibility of creating another prototype chair, in addition to the winning entries, for the MoMA exhibition, using fiberglass. Charles met company executives to discuss the adaptability of the moldable material to furniture. Together they developed the technology for a one-piece armchair that flowed in a single curve of exposed fiberglass, and a full-scale prototype was produced by hand in time to be shown alongside the other Eames prototypes at the MoMA show of winning entries.

1949 ‣ Herman Miller Showroom
8806 Beverly Boulevard, West Hollywood, California

Facing page:
Furniture and accessory arrangements on floor of Herman Miller Showroom

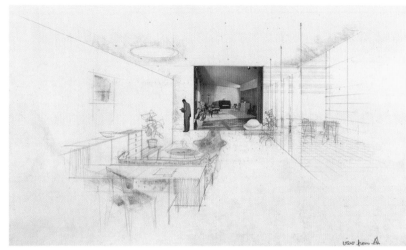

Perspective drawing of the interior of the 1949 Showroom
Pencil on paper with photo collage. The space was designed to serve as a backdrop to enhance the furniture it displayed.

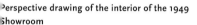

Exterior of the Herman Miller Showroom, designed by Charles and Ray Eames

In the fall of 1949 the Herman Miller Furniture Company Showroom opened its doors at 8806 Beverly Boulevard in West Hollywood. Herman Miller had been selling Eames furniture since 1946, when the unique molded plywood designs featured at an exhibition at MoMA were seen by Herman Miller's director of design George Nelson, who convinced D. J. De Pree, the president of Herman Miller Furniture, of the enormous commercial potential of the Eameses' work. Eventually Herman Miller bought out the Evans Products Company, which was producing the Eames plywood line, and thus acquired the production rights to the furniture. Charles Eames soon became a consultant for the firm.

The design philosophy for the new Herman Miller Showroom was that it was to be a minimalist structure that served primarily as a background to promote the sale of the furniture arrangements displayed on its floors. The industrial steel frame building bore a similarity in style to Case Study House #8, but was adapted to fit the needs of a commercial establishment. The two brick side walls were left exposed on the exterior and painted white on the inside of the building, and the front facade was a steel frame set with sash windows and fixed panels of various types of glass. The 5,000-square-foot showroom interior was an adaptable system of 7-foot bays equipped with openings in the floor and ceiling for removable partition panels. Natural light was provided by three 6-foot circular skylights and the glass windows of the front facade. The showroom floor was partitioned by photomural panels and decorated with toys, flowers, plants, and folk art often provided by the Eameses, as well as paintings and sculptures on loan from local art galleries. The objective, as stated in *Eames Design*, was to "create an 'attitude' of home or office by the use of objects and images." In 1976 the Beverly Boulevard showroom closed and the Herman Miller Furniture Company moved to the new Cesar Pelli-designed Pacific Design Center on Melrose Avenue.

1950 ▸ Storage Units

Eames Storage Units with sliding "dimpled"
front panels

The *Eames Storage Units* (*ESU*) embody all the basic tenets of Eames design: sleek
minimalism, practicality, affordability, industrial materials, and a deeply intelligent use
of outer and inner surfaces. Following a process of natural selection, the ESU evolved
from the pioneering all-plywood modular units that were part of the Charles Eames
and Eero Saarinen winning entry for the 1940 MoMA "Organic Design in Home
Furnishings" exhibition and developed into the "Case Goods" portion of the exhibition
"New Furniture Designed by Charles Eames" at the Museum in 1946. It was at MoMA's
1949 "An Exhibition for Modern Living" that the new and improved version of the
Eames Storage Units was put on public display. In 1950 the *Eames Storage Units* were
presented at the Herman Miller Furniture Company's Beverly Boulevard showroom
where an installation of the units displayed diverse settings and storage options suitable for home or office use. The versatility of the units allowed for a variety of combinations and could be easily adapted to the customer's individual design needs.

The furniture was available in interchangeable single or double-bay units; the 100
series single-bay unit was 20 $5/8$ inches high, 24 inches wide, and 16 inches deep; the
200 series double-bay was 2 units high and 47 inches wide; and the 400 series was a

Configurations of the *Eames Storage Units* system on the Herman Miller Showroom floor

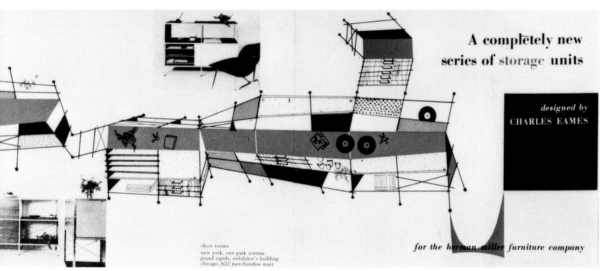

A completely new
series of storage units

designed by
CHARLES EAMES

show rooms
new york, one park avenue
grand rapids, exhibitor's building
chicago, 622 merchandise mart

for the herman miller furniture company

Herman Miller advertisement, c. 1950

units high. Desks with drawers and a filing system completed the line. The standardized cabinet pieces were constructed of chrome-plated steel framing with diagonal rod bracing, and plywood drawers and shelf tops were offered in black plastic laminate or $^3/_4$-inch plywood finished with a choice of birch or walnut. Infill panels of $^1/_8$-inch Masonite came in eight colors, such as primary red, blue, and yellow. Other components of the line included sliding doors of vacuum-pressed dimpled wood and white glass cloth and decorative back panels of perforated metal. The units were shipped in separate components, requiring assembly, but when that proved to be difficult for the consumer the "knockdown" version was replaced with a fully assembled product. The large box the furniture was shipped in was designed by the Eameses to be transformed into a children's playhouse and a pamphlet of instructions for this conversion was enclosed. Although the *Eames Storage Units* were the first modular cabinets to be mass-produced they were not a huge success and were therefore discontinued in 1955.

Window display designed by Eames Office staff member Herbert Matter

Ray Eames' drawings for the stunning 1950 Carson Pirie Scott department store window display in Chicago were a culmination of her years of training as an artist in New York, and featured the three-dimensional spatial tension and brilliant color sense that informed everything she did. Charles Eames had been invited to submit a design for the department store, along with three other leading modernist designers: Eero Saarinen, George Nelson, and Edward Wormley. The stated parameters of the installation were that the furniture displayed had to be examples of the designers' recent work; that it fit the prescribed dimensions of the window; and that it could be set up by the Carson Pirie Scott staff. Ray's proposal took all three requirements into consideration and she used them to help shape her design, which she presented to the department store staff in the form of her sketches and an $^1/_8$-inch scale model. The finished window display comprised a collage of paper and shadows projecting an oversize version of the Eames molded plywood side chair onto the walls. Also in the display and adding to its painterly composition were other carefully selected and strategically placed objects including a table, a group of folding screens, a sculpture, the Herman Miller logo, and a photograph of Charles Eames.

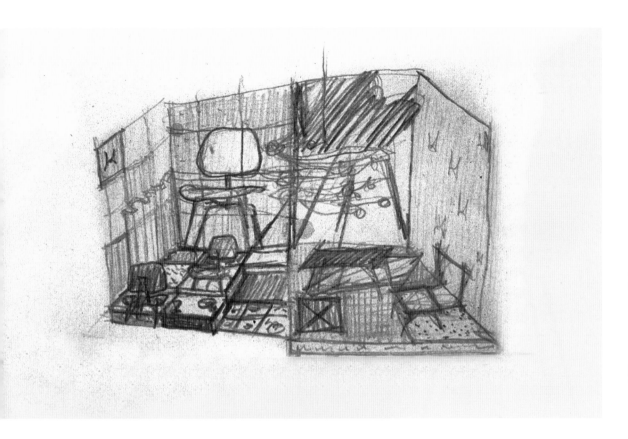

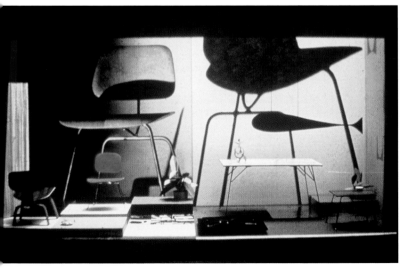

Rough sketch by Ray
The commission for the window displays by the Chicago department store signaled the growing acceptance of modern furniture by the average consumer.

Silhouette and shadow blend to create an emblematic Eamesian design for a window display featuring furniture manufactured by Herman Miller

The continuing saga of the Eames chairs took a dramatic turn when the "plastics" technology of World War II became available to the postwar world. Developed by the U. S. Air Force, polyester plastic reinforced with fiberglass was a "wonder" material that the Eames Office wanted to use for furniture production. Their first fiberglass armchair was developed as a prototype for the 1948 MoMA "International Competition for Low-Cost Furniture Design." Built at Zenith Plastics using the latest tooling technology, including the hydraulic dies used for boat building, the chairs were constructed of the same material the company had used during the war to make fiberglass-reinforced plastic radar domes, and represented the first commercial use of plastic for seating. In Eames Demetrios' *An Eames Primer* Irv Green of Zenith Plastics describes the Eameses' involvment in the process. "They came out to the plant and worked with me, two or three evenings until midnight. This was in Gardena. We molded chair after chair until they finally thought they had what they wanted, and then we put that one aside." This was a gratifying moment for the Eameses because they had finally achieved their goal of mass-producing molded compound curve furniture at prices the average person could afford.

The Herman Miller Furniture Company ordered 2,000 of the fiberglass armchairs from Zenith and offered them for sale in 1950. The natural marbled fiberglass came in parchment, gray, and beige, and later the palette was expanded to include the primary colors. An interchangeable selection of six bases—wooden legs, metal-rod legs, the "Eiffel Tower" wire struts, a cast-aluminum pedestal with casters, a swivel style, and a rocker version with birch rockers on wire struts—gave the customer the opportunity to choose according to their own particular needs. All the bases were attached to the chairs with rubber shock mounts to provide added resiliency. The fiberglass armchair received immediate recognition when it was added in 1950 to MoMA's permanent collection.

With the tooling in place for the plastic armchair, the stamped-metal side chair from the 1948 MoMA exhibition was the next to be converted to fiberglass and added to the Herman Miller Furniture line. Made of a material called Zenaloy, the side chair shell was destined to become a future Eames icon, and was eventually used in schools, airports, restaurants, and offices all over the world. Utilizing metal bars to attach them, the ubiquitous chairs were used for *Stadium Seating* beginning in 1954; *Tandem Shell Seating* in 1963; and *School Seating*, with tablet arms, in 1964. The chair was available with the same six bases as the fiberglass armchair. It could be ordered in natural fiberglass or infused with colors, including black, red, yellow, blue, and green. Hopsacking upholstery, held in place with a wire sewn around the edge of the chair, could be ordered in the same primary colors or in a harlequin pattern.

Also in 1950 the *Low Table Rod Base* (LTR), a small occasional table made of $3/4$-inch plywood and beveled at the edges to expose the plywood layers, was added to the line. Available with a natural wood veneer top, or a laminate surface in black or white, the table was supported by a base constructed of two U-shaped metal rods that were cross-

Plastic side chair variations developed by the Eames Office for production by Zenith Plastics

braced for stability. In 1951 the same base was used at each end of the *Elliptical Table Rod Base* (*ETR*). The spectacular 89-inch-long coffee table looked like an elegant version of a surfboard with a black plastic laminate top that had been set down in the middle of the living room. Only ten inches high, the coffee table invited a Japanese-style seating arrangement on the floor around its base. The table was manufactured for Herman Miller until 1964.

In 1961 the Eameses' *La Fonda Group* featured two chairs similar in shape to the 1951 plastic armchair and side chair. Designed for the La Fonda del Sol restaurant in New York City, the reinforced fiberglass shells of the restaurant chairs were supported on a four-column cast-aluminum pedestal base.

Above, from left to right:
Plastic armchair with wood and wire base; Upholstered drafting armchair; a Saul Steinberg original, drawn during a visit to the Eames Office

Fiberglass armchairs on cat's cradle bases. Shown with a Low Table Rod Base (LTR)

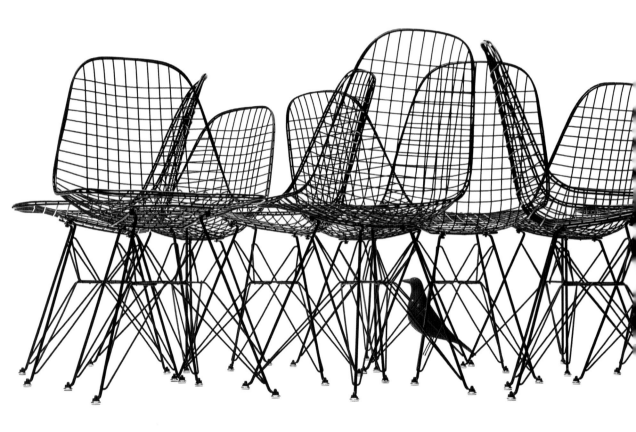

1951–1953 ‣ Wire-Mesh Chairs

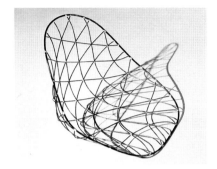

ght:
ent and welded-wire uni-shell mock-up

ar right:
arly wire-welding form used for prototype
ases

artially upholstered *Bikini* model with
n *Eiffel Tower* base from contemporary
roduction

"If you looked around you found these fantastic things being made of wire—trays, baskets, rat traps—using a wire fabricating technique perfected over a period of many years," Ray Eames said in a 1958 *Interiors* magazine article. "We looked into it and found that it was a good production technique and also a good use of material." The wire-mesh chair that evolved between 1951 and 1953 was a logical extension of the process the office was involved in, from the many molded plywood permutations, to the experimental chairs of stamped metal for the 1948 MoMA competition, to the innovative use of industrial technology in the fiberglass chairs, to the new material that formed a lacy web of open woven black wire into a chair like a miniature Eiffel Tower.

The shell of the wire-mesh chair is the same shape as the plastic side chair, and designed to fit the same selection of six separate bases. The Eames Office, experienced in the resistance-welding technique used for their metal-rod bases, applied the same methods to construct the wire chair, weaving the metal into small squares for strength in the center, surrounded by open horizontal lines at the outer edges. The rim of the chair is made of a heavier gauge wire that is doubled to increase overall strength and stability. The Eames Office was awarded the first American mechanical patent for the design of this inventive solution.

The chair was available in three configurations; fully upholstered; partially upholstered with padding that formed triangular bases on the seat and back of the chair (known today as the *Bikini* model); or with no upholstery at all. Materials included black or tan glove leather, vinyl, tan cotton, tweed hopsacking, and a harlequin print. Manufactured by Banner Metals of Compton, California, the wire-mesh chairs were marketed by Herman Miller from 1951 to 1967, and reintroduced by the furniture company in 2001.

acing page:
dvertising photograph for wire-mesh
hairs with a blackbird sculpture, c. 1952

1952 ▸ House of Cards

The joyous sensibility that Charles and Ray Eames brought to their work is perhaps best illustrated in their lifelong affiliation with toys. "We have to take pleasure seriously," an often used quote attributed to Charles Eames, exemplifies the work/play ethic that contributed so profoundly to all that they did. Toys informed their existence, in the eclectic and whimsical collection of objects appearing like a leitmotif in their home, their workplace, and in their numerous films and exhibitions. Toys were also created by the Eames Office for mass production, from the children's playhouse to be converted from an *ESU* shipping box, to *The Toy*, containing geometric paper panels for assemblage. One of the most stunningly innovative and commercially successful of these ventures was the *House of Cards*.

Distributed in 1952 by the Chicago toy firm Tigrett Enterprises and printed by American Playing Cards, the *House of Cards* was a deck of 54 regulation-size cards with illustrations on one side and an asterisk on a white background on the other. Each card had six slots, one on each end and two on each side, that could be interlocked to allow infinite spatial architectural variations. Two versions were distributed by Tigrett in 1952, first the *Pattern Deck*, soon followed by the *Picture Deck*. Illustrations for both decks reflected the beauty to be found in the natural world and in the nostalgia of everyday life. Based on Charles' notion of "good things" chosen from nature, what he designated "the animal, vegetable and mineral world," the selection of images was done in the Eames Office by Ray and staff members, including Alexander Girard, who made the final decisions on the chosen designs for the cards.

The *Pattern Deck* was stacked with examples of graphic designs, textured paper; printed fabrics, an old-fashioned nosegay, a turkey feather, and a Chinese foil butterfly. The reverse side of this deck had a gray-green asterisk on a white background. The *Picture Deck* united disparate items, including a cigar box, a toy car, train, and railroad station, a metronome, a snail shell on sand, a Native-American Kachina doll, and an assortment of household items, such as scissors, straight pins, thread, and a thimble. Its reverse side had a black asterisk on a white background. When fitted together into various three-dimensional structures, the *House of Cards* became a cardboard kaleidoscope of constantly changing color. Both decks were sold together in Eames-designed packaging.

Another version of the *House of Cards* designed by the Eames Office was the 1953 *Giant House of Cards*, consisting of twenty cards made of eight-ply cardboard that measured seven by eleven inches each and were also slotted for interlocking. Images included a halftone print of an eggshell, an enlargement of snowflakes, a nautilus shell, gemstones, a spiral, and a collection of old watch movements. The reverse sides featured dazzling primary colors bordered with white. In 1970 the *Computer House of Cards* was printed exclusively as a souvenir of the IBM Pavilion Exhibition organized by the Eames Office at the World's Fair in Osaka, Japan.

1951 ▸ Kwikset House

Living room of the Kwikset model with *Storage Units*

One-inch model of the Kwikset House

Although never built, the Kwikset House was a powerful prototype of postwar housing designed to fill the country's need for low-cost homes that were prefabricated and could be assembled from a kit of modular off-the-shelf parts on the building site. The Kwikset Lock Company, advertisers in *Arts & Architecture* and suppliers of hardware for the Case Study Houses, commissioned the Eames Office in 1951 to design a house that could be successfully developed for mass production. The one-inch scale model of the single-span concept was reminiscent of the World War II metal Quonset Hut, with a curved roof made of sections of plywood that were supported on curved laminated beams defining the unobstructed central space. The freestanding interior, complete with miniature Eames furniture, had walls that were flexible and could be adapted according to the needs of the homeowner into variable arrangements of a living room, a dining room, two bedrooms, and a kitchen. The metal framework of the front facade was fitted with glass panels and doors. The Kwikset House reflected the Eameses' philosophy of interactive standardized modules to be used in variant forms. When the Kwikset Lock Company was sold the new management decided against the project and it was never realized.

1954 ▸ Max De Pree House
Zeeland, Michigan

xterior view

The brief for the Max De Pree House in Zeeland, Michigan stated that only local Dutch artisans, many of them trained in the Netherlands, were to be hired for its construction. As a result of their specialized skills, the timber frame structure was built with hand-tooled accuracy and precision. Max De Pree was the son of D. J. De Pree, a Dutch businessman and chairman of the Herman Miller Furniture Company, which had been affiliated with the Eames Office since 1946. The young scion wanted a contemporary house, set on this open tree-lined site, that would reflect Scandinavian esthetics and adapt gracefully to the neighborhood's cultural ambience. The Eames Office, headed by Don Albinson, designed a two-story rectangular house with an open plan somewhat akin to the Case Study Houses in California, but with a minimum use of glass because of the cold Michigan winters. The roof was flat with an overhang that was reiterated in the second story balcony at the front and back of the house. The front facade featured strong vertical elements in a modular grid with infills of wood and glass. The interiors were also designed by the Eames Office. Included in the original plans were blueprints for various room additions, all of which the De Prees implemented over the years, before selling the house in 1975 to the Rynbrandt family.

1956 ▸ Lounge Chair and Ottoman

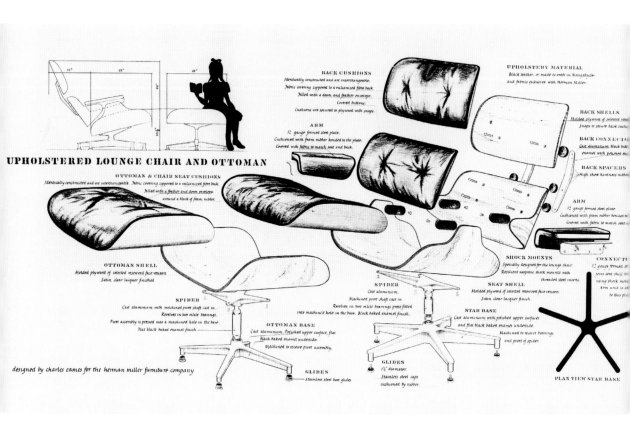

Diagram of *Chair and Ottoman* components, with calligraphy by Sister Corita Kent of the Immaculate Heart College

Diagram of *Chair and Ottoman* components, with calligraphy by Sister Corita Kent of the Immaculate Heart College

Architectural historian Esther McCoy said, "No other piece of furniture has so stirred the mind and heart of the twentieth century both here and abroad."

For Charles and Ray Eames immortality has come in the shape of chairs and of them all the most iconic is the 1956 wood and leather *Lounge Chair and Ottoman*. Its histo goes back to the 1940 MoMA show "Organic Design in Home Furnishings." Amor the prototypes submitted for the competition by Charles Eames and Eero Saarinen wa a lounge chair with modern esthetics that offered the comfort of a traditional armcha This first chair was far from perfect in Charles' mind, but it was the shape of things come. In 1945 and 1946 Charles and Ray worked on an experimental lounge chair mad of three large sections of curving molded plywood that was never produced. Sever versions of the chair were created, each one a learning experience moving closer to th design solution the Eameses sought. As Charles so famously said, he wanted the cha to have the "warm, receptive look of a well-used first baseman's mitt."

A decade later, in 1956, the first prototype of the chair that fit like a glove was give to film director Billy Wilder, a close friend of the Eameses. The first run of fifty chai fabricated for the Herman Miller Showroom was mechanically tooled and then pu together by hand. A Herman Miller executive arranged for the chair's debut on nation television, on the "Home Show" hosted by Arlene Francis. Charles prepared for the T

66

Profile of *Lounge Chair and Ottoman*

show a two-minute film demonstrating the manufacture, assembly, and packing process of the new chair, with background music by Elmer Bernstein.

Although the chair sold for $404, a high price at the time, it was an immediate bestseller. By 1975 Herman Miller had sold 100,000. Because the chair required a combination of factory tooling and hand craftsmanship it was expensive to produce, and was a departure from the Eameses' ethos of affordable furniture for the people. Composed of three curved plywood shells made of rosewood, the *Lounge Chair* was padded with buttoned black leather upholstery filled with foam, down, and duck feathers. The *Ottoman*, a single-curved shell, was similarly padded. Rubber shock mounts, used for connections, provided resiliency and flexibility. The swivel base, a five-star "spider" mechanism on which the chair and the *Ottoman* rotated, was made of cast aluminum available with a polished or black matte finish. The *Lounge Chair and Ottoman*, unchanged except for a new filling made of dacron and foam and the rosewood replaced with walnut, is still in the Herman Miller catalog and is currently selling for $3,500 with the *Ottoman*.

1957 ‣ Film: Day of the Dead

Stills of the 14.48 minute color film

Day of the Dead, or All Souls' Day, is celebrated in Mexico on November 1, and Charles Eames experienced the religious festival firsthand during his nine-month Mexican sojourn in 1933. He had left St. Louis in frustration over his languishing Depression-era career to try and find himself as a stranger in a strange land. While traveling around the Mexican countryside he absorbed with an artist's eye the native culture on its own terms, painting landscapes and village churches, which he sold to support himself. He collected indigenous trinkets, folk art, and fabrics that anticipated a lifelong interest in objects. This was the backdrop for *Day of the Dead*, a 1957 fifteen-minute color film that combined the annual All Souls' Day procession and a powerful selection of representative artifacts to tell the story of an ancient cultural event.

By 1957 the Eames Office had produced several short films, including their first film, *Traveling Boy*, shot in 1951 with a rented 16 mm camera in the Eames House

studio, which was never shown; the 1952 *Blacktop*, a visually elegant study of water on a schoolyard playground, which won the Edinburgh International Film Festival Award in 1954; and the nostalgic *House—After Five Years of Living*, a film made by Charles and Ray of their beloved Eames House in 1955. Both produced over a hundred films in their lifetime, for exhibitions, corporations, demonstrations, and general release. All of them featured compelling combinations of rapid cutting, animation, still shots, and live action designed to capture the viewer's attention and disseminate information.

Day of the Dead used many of these techniques to create a combination of live action sequences, footage shot from 35 mm slides that were transferred to film, and a series of frames taken from 16 mm film footage of the colorful folk objects the villagers created for the festival. The text was written by Charles Eames with Edgar Kauffman, Jr., and Alexander Girard, the music was composed and performed by guitarist Laurindo Almeida.

1958 ▸ Aluminum Group

Above:
Charles and Ray exploring ideas for upholstering the sling seat of the aluminum chair

Below:
Eames Office staff at work on a prototype for the aluminum chair

When Alexander Girard, a longtime staff member of the Eames Office, had trouble finding suitable indoor-outdoor furniture for a house he was working on with Eero Saarinen in Columbus, Ohio, he discussed with Charles the possibility of a new line of quality leisure furniture that would fill the gap. Girard, who was designing the house's interior, wanted furniture that was light enough to move outdoors and strong enough to resist the corrosive effects of the elements. For the 1948 MoMA "International Competition for Low-Cost Furniture Design" the Eames Office had worked with aluminum for their metal-stamping process, using sheets of the material to stamp out prototype chairs. Familiar with its properties, the Office began experimenting with cast aluminum for a new line of what was to be leisure furniture.

The use of aluminum for furniture dated back to before World War II. It had been used by designers such as Marcel Breuer and Hans Coray in the United States and Europe in the 1930s, and in 1933 aluminum chairs were the subject of an international competition in Paris, France. During the war aluminum was pressed into military service, where it was refined, strengthened, and lowered in cost, making it far more marketable to the postwar world. The aluminum companies promoted its use and in 1957 Alcoa hired several well-known graphic designers, including the Eameses, to help put the material on the map. Charles and Ray devised a beautiful, intricate aluminum toy, the *Solar Do-Nothing Machine*, which used photovoltaic cells to explore the potential of aluminum and solar energy and served as a prestigious advertisement for Alcoa.

A series of full-scale mock-ups of aluminum chairs was developed at the Eameses' 901 Washington Boulevard office over a three-year period. What emerged from the assiduous process was the furniture that was to become known as the *Aluminum Group*

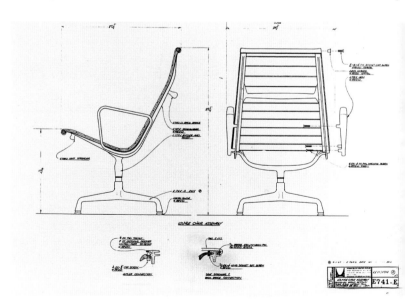

Aluminum Group specification drawings

he star of which was the high-back, tilt-swivel lounge chair. Aluminum "antlers" across the back and under the seat connected the two brightly polished metallic side frames of the chair, and a continuous piece of upholstery was slung across the frame and lightly rolled over aluminum bars at the top and the bottom. The upholstery consisted of a laminated "sandwich" of two-sided Naughahyde filled with nylon and vinyl foam that was bonded together and ribbed at 1 $^7/_8$-inch intervals. The chair's "sling" seat esthetics was reminiscent of a hammock, or of the 1938 *Butterfly Chair* which was still popular in the 1950s, perhaps reflecting the Eameses' original intention of designing casual indoor-outdoor furniture. Available in the *Aluminum Group* was a group of high- and low-back lounge chairs, with or without arms, all supported on swivel cast aluminum bases; a matching ottoman also on a swivel base; a dining table and dining chairs; and coffee tables with a choice of slate, glass, or Botticino marble tops.

Aluminum Group production model

Eleven years later the Eames Office came out with the *Soft Pad Group*, a line of furniture that was a structural offshoot of its predecessor, the *Aluminum Group*. The original 1969 *Soft Pad* chairs came in black leather with polished aluminum frames, and consisted of a low-back side chair, a high-back executive chair, two lounge chairs, and an ottoman. A stretched membrane of upholstery, similar to the "laminated sandwich" of the aluminum lounge chair, was covered with seat cushions and rectangular soft pads, two on the side chair and three on the executive chair. Filling for the zippered cushions consisted of two-inch-thick foam wrapped in fiber batting. All the chairs were supported on cast-aluminum pedestal-swivel bases with casters. A three-screen slide show explaining the construction process of the chairs was expanded with live action footage into a four-minute demonstration film for the Herman Miller Showroom in 1970.

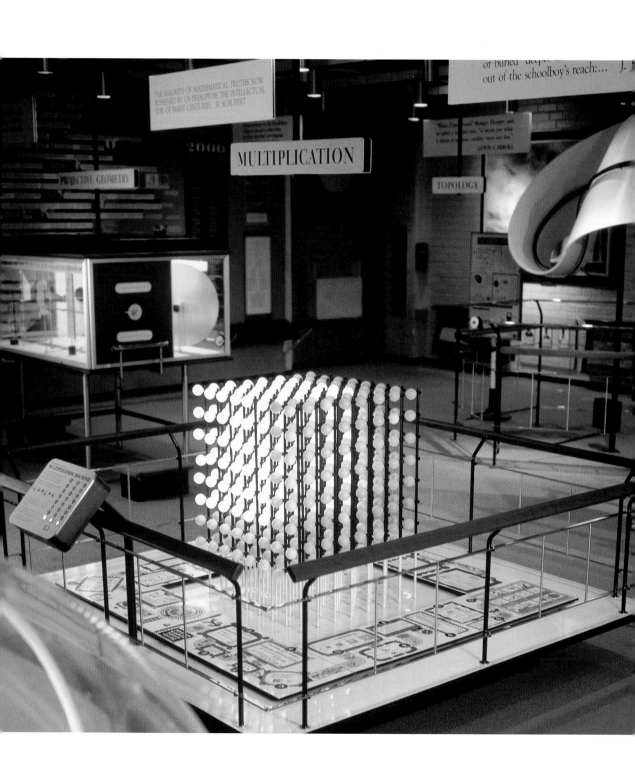

1961 ▸ Exhibition: Mathematica

The first concept exhibition designed by the Eames Office was an extravaganza of scientific information transformed into intellectual entertainment. Visitors to "Mathematica: A World of Numbers and Beyond" entered a theme park of fundamental math problems and their solutions conveyed by means of graphic panels, demonstrations, and explanatory interactive devices. When the California Museum of Science and Industry planned to open a new science wing in 1961 they approached the IBM Company to sponsor a display. IBM Corporation, which had already worked with the Eameses on several films, commissioned the Eames Office to conceive a suitable exhibition.

With consultant Ray Redheffer, a UCLA mathematics professor, the Eameses researched the project for a year, building an early quarter-inch scale study model and then a more complete half-inch scale model of the planned exhibition space. The allotted 3,000-square-foot area in the Museum's new science wing was used to present science as engagingly as possible and to entertain as well as educate the public. Two 50-foot-long walls were key features of the exhibition, one a "History Wall," a timeline of progress outlined within the lifespans of famous mathematicians, and the other an "Image Wall" of graphics, photographs, and diagrams interpreting mathematical principles.

A sign over the showcase model at the entrance to the exhibition read, "Take a good look at these models—it can suggest the richness and vitality within the discipline of mathematics." Translating the rigors of math for the general public was a prime objective of the Eames Office, and Charles, in keeping with his philosophy of "serious fun," wanted to "let the fun out of the bag" for the show and "follow all of the rules of the concept involved." This he did in the central area of the exhibition, which was filled with nine interactive displays on subjects including multiplication, topology, celestial mechanics, projective geometry, and probability. Visitors had the opportunity to

Showcase model of projective geometry

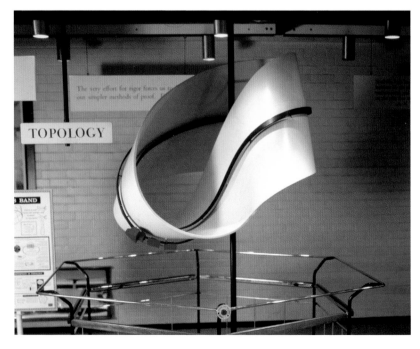

The *Moebius Band*

Lucia Eames Demetrios and daughter Lucia look through viewing devices at the exhibition's "peep shows"

Charles and Ray working on a conceptual model of the exhibition layout

"activate" the scientific principles of each subject by pushing a button. The *Multiplication Cube* clarified the functions of squaring and cubing; rotating spheres in the Celestial Mechanics device went into elliptical orbits; and the *Moebius Band* was interpreted with a traveling red arrow.

Five "peep shows" composed mostly of animation created by Eames Office staff member Glen Fleck, and written by Fleck and Charles Eames, with music by film composer Elmer Bernstein, were two-minute instructional presentations on subjects including functions, symmetry, and topology. The peep shows were shown on devices for single viewers, then moved to small theaters, and finally removed from the show because of the technical difficulties of repeated viewings.

The Eames Office exhibitions were power-packed, visually and viscerally exciting learning experiences designed to inform the general public. Subjects were diverse and included "Good Design" in 1951; "Nehru: His Life and His India" in 1965; "Photography & the City" in 1968; the IBM Pavilion at the 1964–1965 World's Fair in New York City; and "The World of Franklin and Jefferson" in 1975. In 1961 a reproduction of the "Mathematica" exhibition was installed at the Chicago Museum of Science and Industry. It ran until 1980, when it was moved to the Boston Museum of Science. The exhibition, which has become an exemplar for scientific presentations everywhere, can still be seen at its original venue, the California Museum of Science and Industry in Los Angeles.

1962 ▸ Tandem Sling Seating

In the late 1950s the Eames Office was approached by two architectural firms, Eero Saarinen Associates and C. F. Murphy Associates, to design public seating for new terminals at Dulles Airport in Washington, DC, and Chicago's O'Hare Airport. Flying was becoming a popular way to travel and new airport facilities were being built to accommodate the growing number of passengers. Both airports wanted a multiple seating system for their buildings, and they wanted a system that was Eames-designed. The Eames Office had already experimented with *Stadium Seating* in 1954, using their fiberglass armchair and side chair shells fastened in a row to a steel beam. Although it never got beyond the prototype stage, *Stadium Seating*, the product of years of study and research, became the template for the 1962 Eames *Tandem Sling Seating*.

Applying the technology learned for the *Aluminum Sling Chair*, the new chair for tandem seating retained the polished aluminum frames, but the one-piece sling was replaced by separate interchangeable seat and back pads that could be easily changed. Durability, strength, and resistance to wear and tear were essential qualities for chairs that would have such heavy use, and the production models built at the Eames Office were sent to the Herman Miller Technical Center in Zeeland, Michigan. There they underwent a series of stringent tests, including a model seat pad subjected to a 100-pound weight dropped 15,000 times from a height of five inches onto its surface, to assess their durability. Single or double rows of the chairs were attached to a continuous steel T-beam, in interlocking sets of two to ten chairs. The seat pads had the same sandwich construction as the *Aluminum Sling Chair*, with black or colored Naugahyde enclosing vinyl foam and nylon in a heat-sealed package. Instead of the rectangular ribbing of the *Aluminum Sling Chair* the chair pads' laminated lines formed geometric patterns.

Herman Miller began production of the chairs in 1962 and the system was installed at Dulles and O'Hare airports, soon to be followed by installations at airports the world over. The concept of multiple public seating was continued in 1963 with *Tandem Shell Seating*, using the Eames plastic armchair and side chair shells attached to cast-aluminum "spiders" mounted onto a black steel T-beam. In 1964 *School Seating* was addressed by the Eames Office, with multiple seating units made of their fiberglass shells mounted in rows on black steel straps.

1964–1965 ▸ IBM Pavilion
New York World's Fair

Elevated 90 feet above the translucent central canopy of the Pavilion, the Ovoid Theater was the main attraction at the IBM exhibition of the 1964–1965 World's Fair in New York City. A spectacular "People Wall" raised and lowered as many as 400 fair visitors at a time in its bleacher seats into the Ovoid's interior, where the Eames-produced documentary *Think* was projected onto twenty screens of assorted shapes and sizes. Film sequences, presented in the mixed media of animation, stills, and live action, sought to demonstrate the commonality of ordinary problems—planning a dinner party, weather prediction, coaching football—and the similar problem-solving methods used in computer processing. The purpose of the 30-minute film was to welcome viewers to the computer age and dispel some of its mystery.

Charles Eames and Eero Saarinen had been commissioned by the IBM Corporation to design an exhibition on a 1.2 acre site on the fair grounds in Flushing Meadows, New York. When Saarinen died in the fall of 1961 the Eames Office continued the collaboration with Saarinen Associates. Early discussions between Eames and Saarinen established a goal of focusing on a visitor's experience of the exhibition rather than on the Pavilion's architectural aspects. "From any approach the visitor looks through trees and shrubs into an open and spacious structure," Charles said in a project presentation film. "The supporting elements are so developed that they are not unlike the natural forms themselves." To implement this concept a grove of 45 "Corten" steel trees, 32 feet high with spans up to 35 feet across, became the "supporting elements" for the several opaque plastic canopies that covered a garden of exhibition areas. These areas continued the theme of demystifying the computer and defining its use in everyday life.

The Eames Office produced three computer-generated puppet shows for the Fair, titled *Computer Day at Midvale*, *Cast of Characters*, and *Sherlock Holmes and the Singular Case of the Plural Green Mustache*, all of which were electronic vehicles to familiarize fairgoers with computers and data processing. A "Computer Court" demonstrated the principles underlying an IBM data processing machine and "The Typewriter Bar" invited visitors to try out the latest equipment. Two of the elements from the IBM "Mathematica" show were replicated for the Fair; the "Scholar's Walk," lined with rectangular graphic panels collaged with cartoons, photographs, and mathematicians' thoughts and anecdotes, and a 14-foot "Probability Machine."

At the conclusion of the World's Fair in the fall of 1965 the buildings and exhibits of the IBM Pavilion were dismantled. Films produced by the Eames Office to commemorate the World's Fair exhibition and record it for posterity were *IBM at the Fair*, 1965, a short film with fast cuts, time lapses, high-speed photography, and a score by Elmer Bernstein; *View from the People Wall*, 1966, composite fragments from the *Think* documentary presented in 16 mm film on a single screen; and two of the computer-generated puppet shows combined into a single instructional film.

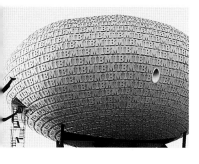

1968 ▸ Exhibition: Photography & the City

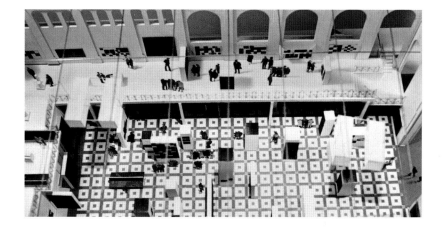

"Photography & the City" was designed by the Eames Office to examine the role photography plays in determining the progressive development of a city. Installed in 1968 in the Arts & Industries Building of the Smithsonian Institution in Washington, DC, the exhibition featured photographs selected from the Smithsonian and the Library of Congress archives, and from collections in the United States and Europe.

The work of such legendary photographers as Alfred Stieglitz, Dorothea Lange, Louis Jacques Mandé (Daguerre), Jacob Riis, and Lewis Hine illustrated the role of the photographic image in the urban setting, from the historic beginnings in an 1905 study of immigrants at Ellis Island to a contemporary composition of the skyscrapers of New York City. The images, printed and mounted at the Eames Office in Venice, were displayed singly and as composite photo murals on freestanding rectangular pylons. The graphic pylons divided the spacious central court of the Arts & Industries Building into the subject areas of architecture and planning, photojournalism, mapmaking, social documentation, aerial photography, and photojournalism. Vintage cameras and other historic photographic equipment in artifact cases completed the exhibition. "Photography & the City" opened on June 6, 1968, and ran until January 1, 1969.

1972 ▸ Film: Banana Leaf

A sequence of frames was chosen from 16 mm film footage to tell a story of relative values.

The Eameses' fascination with all things Indian began in 1955 when they made a film of MoMA's "Textiles and Ornamental Arts of India," an exhibition on Indian culture designed by their friends Alexander Girard and Edgar Kauffman, Jr. Through the medium of film Charles wanted to preserve the exhibition and make it accessible to a larger audience. The visually rich footage used long shots and close-ups of the galleries to present an overview of Indian artifacts and culture. While shooting the film Charles and Ray became friends with Mrs. Pupul Jayakar, an official with the Indian Ministry of Commerce and Industry, who later invited them to prepare what Charles called a "position paper" on the effect of Western technology on Indian culture.

In 1957 Charles and Ray traveled to India, touring the countryside and observing the lifestyle, meeting people from all walks of life, and photographing everything of interest they saw. The resulting "Eames India Report" recommended the establishment of an "Institute of Design Research and Service," a design center that would produce books, exhibitions, and television programs on contemporary cultural issues for the Indian government. In 1961 the National Institute of Design (NID) was founded in Ahmadabad, an organization that worked closely with the Eames Office over the ensuing years. In 1964 Indira Gandhi, whose father, Prime Minister Jawaharlal Nehru, had recently died, commissioned the Eameses to plan a traveling exhibition as a memorial to her father's contributions to his country, and in 1965 and 1966 "Nehru: His Life and His India" toured venues in London, New York, Washington, DC, Los Angeles, and Delhi.

This immersion in Indian culture led to an abiding interest of the Eameses, reflected in the short 1972 film *Banana Leaf*, an examination of an Indian parable based on the caste system that Charles often used to make a point about relative values in his lectures. In a December 1971 address to the American Association for the Advancement of Science Charles told the story thus: "The very poor man in India eats his meal off a banana leaf. A little higher in the scale is a low-fired earthenware dish, a tali. Then a glazed tali, then brass, then bell bronze, or polished marble, which are both very handsome—then to show you can do better than that, you get into things that are rather questionable: silver plate, solid silver—presumably even gold. But there are some superior men—with not only means but understanding, and probably some spiritual training as well—who will go a step further and eat off a banana leaf." In the film's beginning a peasant is depicted eating his meal from a banana leaf. The various other stages or castes are depicted leading to the ending frames showing a high-caste priest back to eating his meal from a banana leaf. Shot in live action, the film was written and narrated by Charles Eames. The unreleased film has been transferred to video.

Facing page:
The simplest and at the same time most refined version of a dish: the banana leaf

1977 ▸ Film: Powers of Ten

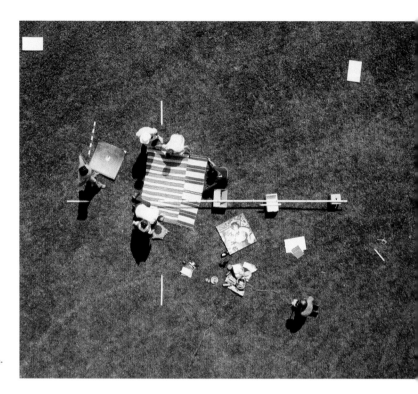

Arranging the picnic scene for the opening shot of the 1977 *Powers of Ten* on the field behind the Eames Office at 901 Washington Boulevard
On the lawn an enlarged photo of the original set-up from the 1968 version was used as a guide.

Powers of Ten is the most celebrated of all the Eames films and is considered to be the most hauntingly profound. There are two versions, the 1968 black-and-white *Powers of Ten: A Rough Sketch for a Proposed Film Dealing with the Powers of Ten and the Relative Size of the Universe* and the 1977 color *Powers of Ten: A Film Dealing with the Relative Size of Things in the Universe and the Effect of Adding Another Zero*. The 1968 film was an early interpretation of the basic concept which was prepared for the Commission on College Physics added advances in science that had occurred in the nine years between the two.

Charles Eames had read *Cosmic View: The Universe in Forty Jumps*, a 1957 book by Dutch educator Kees Boeke, written for his students at Werkplaats Children's Community, a school in the Netherlands. Boeke's book examined scale through a series of forty painstakingly drawn pictures, all scientifically accurate in their relationship to size and distance, that depicted a journey through space and back again into the interior space of an atom. Scale and the relative size of things were ideas the Eameses had already begun exploring in the 1953 science education film on applied mathematics, *A Communication Primer*, and later in one of the IBM exhibition "Mathematica" peep shows titled "2^n", which used an ancient folktale to explore the notion of exponentiality. As Ray explained in the 1982 book on the film, "Charles learned from

Eero Saarinen the importance of looking at things from the next largest scale and the next smallest."

To watch *Powers of Ten* is to become a traveler in a strange, strange land. The viewer embarks on a thrilling and unnerving journey to the outer reaches of our scientific knowledge, with cosmology at one end of the trip and particle physics at the other. The first version, filmed in 1968 on a Florida golf course, displayed the distance in meters, the passing of time, and the percentage of the speed of light on an instrument panel on the left side of the screen. For the finished 1977 version the panel is removed and the location changed to the shores of Lake Michigan in Chicago. It begins with a 30-second live action sequence depicting a one-meter-square image of an ordinary picnic on an ordinary day. A man lies back and falls asleep on a striped picnic blanket with his hand shielding his eyes from the sun. As the camera begins to pull away from that hand we see that it moves ten times farther away every ten seconds and the fantastic voyage takes the viewer up, up, and away from all things familiar, past the "blue marble" of Earth, past the sun and the Milky Way, past our swirling galaxy and into vast clusters of orbiting galaxies until we reach 10 to the 25th power, the edge of the known universe, the outer limits of our current vision. Now the camera reverses and moves ten times closer each ten seconds as it zooms downward to come to rest for a moment on the sleeping man's hand. Here the mind must adjust to an alternate journey, deep into the interior galaxies of the human body, through the skin, the collagen, the capillaries, red and white blood cells, the cell nucleus, the twisted ladders of DNA, and into the ultimate inner space of a carbon nucleus, an atom, a quark, where the other edge is reached at 10 to the minus 16th power.

The 1968 version of *Powers of Ten* was further developed into the finished 1977 production by the Eames Office assisted by Philip Morrison, an MIT professor of physics, and a brain trust of scientific advisers from disciplines including astrophysics, biology, genetics, and particle physics. Over the period of a year relevant artwork and photographs were assembled and forty representative images were carefully chosen to be repeatedly photographed for the film. To achieve the smooth and realistic motion of an animated film odyssey the photographs were arranged frame-by-frame on a 40-foot-long animation stand, comparable to a giant storyboard, and then turned into the final film. The process was innovative for its time and costly to accomplish but the result was well worth the expense.

Powers of Ten is internationally recognized as a masterpiece and is constantly used as a teaching tool in schools, universities, and museums all over the world. It was completed a year before Charles Eames' death and was his last significant accomplishment. Narrated by physicist Philip Morrison, who in 1982 coauthored with his wife, Phylis Morrison, the book *Powers of Ten* for the Scientific American Library series, the finished film is nine minutes long. The musical score is by Charles and Ray's longtime friend, film composer Elmer Bernstein.

Charles in lift, Ray with camera, and Eames Office staff members studying camera angles of sleeping man on picnic blanket for the 1968 "rough sketch" version of *Powers of Ten*

Powers of Ten visually expands and then contracts the universe as we know it.

100,000 light years

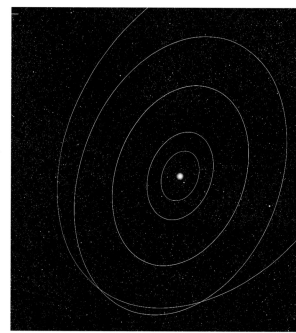

10 billion kilometers

10 kilometers

1 kilometer

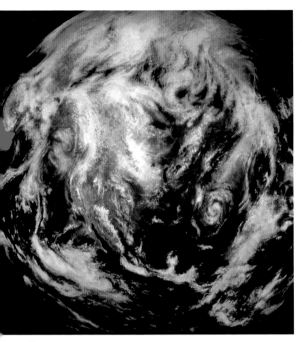

o,ooo kilometers

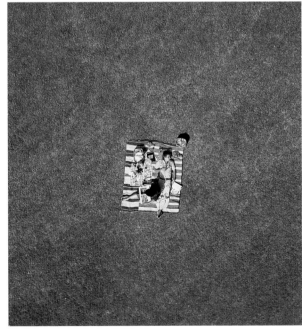

1,000 kilometers

oo meters

10 meters

The 9-minute film is constantly used as
a teaching tool in schools, universities, and
museums in countries all over the world.

1 meter

10 centimeters

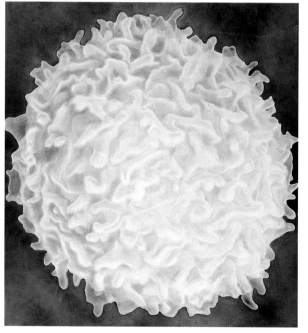

10 microns

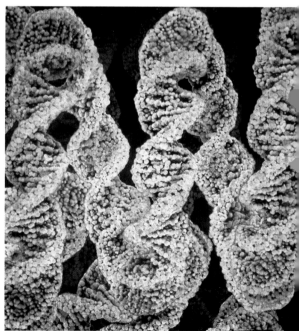

10 nanometers

centimeter

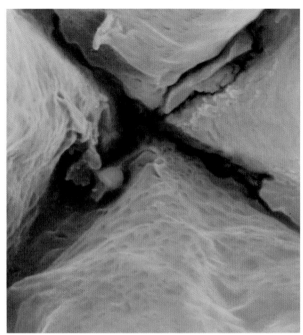

100 microns

nanometer

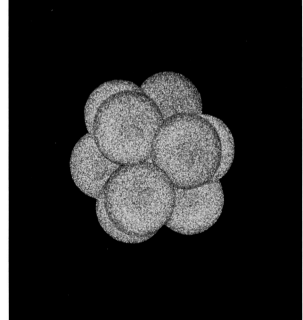

10 fermis

Life and Work

CHARLES EAMES

1907 ▶ Charles Ormond Eames, Jr., born June 17 in St. Louis, Missouri.

1917 ▶ First job at age ten, at a printing shop, Upton S. Cody.

1920 ▶ Discovers father's cache of photographic materials, triggering a lifelong interest in film and photography.

Charles Eames at age fourteen, at Laclede Steel Mill, 1921

1921 ▶ Enters Yeatman High School, St. Louis, Missouri.

1924 ▶ Elected class president and captain of football team.
Receives architecture scholarship at Washington University, St. Louis, Missouri.

1925 ▶ Graduates from Yeatman High School, St. Louis, Missouri.
Enters Washington Uni-versity, elected president of freshman class.
Works for Edwin F. Guth Fixture Co, designs lighting fixtures.

1928 ▶ Leaves Washington University after sophomore year.

1929 ▶ Marriage to Washington University student Catherine Dewey Woermann.
On honeymoon trip to Europe, first sees the work of Mies van der Rohe, Walter Gropius, and Le Corbusier.

1930–1933 ▶ Opens architectural office, Gray & Eames Architects, St. Louis, Missouri, then takes another partner, Gray, Eames & Pauley. Firm designs Sweetzer House, in University City, St. Louis, Missouri, and two houses in Webster Grove, Missouri.

1933 ▶ Pilgrim Congregational Church, St. Louis, Missouri, renovation and design.

1934 ▶ Works for WPA's Historic American Building Survey in St. Louis and New Orleans. Travels and paints in Mexico for eight months.

1935 ▶ Opens new architectural firm, Eames & Walsh. Firm designs St. Mary's Church in Helena, Arkansas, and another church in Paragould, Arkansas. Eliel Saarinen contacts Charles.

1936 ▶ Eames & Walsh design Dinsmoor House in Webster Grove, Missouri, and works with Eero and Eliel Saarinen on the Meyer House. Eliel Saarinen becomes a mentor.

1938–1940 ▶ Cranbrook Academy of Art, in Cranbrook, Michigan. Eliel Saarinen, Cranbrook director, offers Charles a Fellowship. Charles begins in the fall.
Instructor of design in the Intermediate School at Cranbrook in 1939.
Designs faculty exhibition in Cranbrook Pavilion with Eero Saarinen.
Appointed head of Department of Industrial Design at Cranbrook in 1940 and joins Eliel Saarinen's architectural firm that same year. Works with Eero Saarinen on seating design for the Kleinhans Music Hall in Buffalo, New York, and collaborates with him on Cranbrook entry for MoMA's competition "Organic Design in Home Furnishings." Wins first prize.

acing page:
:harles in the Eames House studio with oxes he often assembled to play with his :randchildren

1941 ▸ Charles and Catherine Woermann divorce in May. Charles and Ray Kaiser marry on June 20 in Chicago, Illinois. Charles and Ray drive cross country to Los Angeles, arriving July 5. Charles begins work at MGM Studios in the Art Department.

RAY KAISER

1912 ▸ Bernice Alexandra Kaiser (called Ray-Ray) born December 15 in Sacramento, California.

Charles with a christmas tree made of molded plywood chair legs, c. 1946

1936–1937 ▸ Becomes a founding member of the American Abstract Artists (AAA), New York. Exhibition of Ray's painting at the AAA's first show, at the Riverside Museum, New York.

1940 ▸ Mother dies. Begins attending Cranbrook Academy of the Arts in September. Works with Charles Eames on MoMA competition "Organic Design in Home Furnishings."

1941 ▸ Marries Charles on June 20 in Chicago, Illinois.

CHARLES AND RAY EAMES

1941 ▸ Charles and Ray rent Westwood apartment in Richard Neutra-designed building. Begin experiments with molded plywood chairs. Charles invents the Kazam! machine to facilitate molding process.
An exhibition of prize-winning furniture by Charles Eames and Eero Saarinen from "Organic Design in Home Furnishings" held in September at MoMA in New York.

1942 ▸ Develop molded plywood leg splints for the U.S. Navy and begin production.
Charles leaves MGM to work full time on splints and a molded plywood body litter.
Ray designs six covers for John Entenza's *California Arts & Architecture* magazine.

1943 ▸ Work on molded plywood aircraft parts for Vultee BT15 Trainer. Work on plywood nose section and glider parts for aircraft.
Continue experimentation on molded plywood furniture.
Ray designs ten covers for *Arts & Architecture* magazine.
Painting *For C in Limited Pallette* by Ray.

1944
Article in *Arts & Architecture*, "What Is a House?"
Eight covers designed by Ray for the magazine.
Painting *Composition in Yellow* by Ray.

1945 ▸ Case Study House Program announced in January issue *Arts & Architecture*. Charles Eames and Eero Saarinen design Case Study House #8 as the Eames House and Case Study House #9 for John Entenza.
Slide show: "Lecture 1 at California Institute of Technology"
Molded Plywood Animals, Chairs, and Tables
Children's Furniture
Experimental Chairs

Ray Eames painting an abstract cutout

Ray Kaiser in New York, 1939/1940

1925 ▸ Enters Sutter Junior High School, Sacramento, California.

1931 ▸ Graduates from Sacramento High School. Moves to New York with mother. Enters May Friend Bennett School in the fall.

1933 ▸ Graduates from May Friend Bennett School. Joins Art Students League, New York. Studies painting with German-born artist Hans Hofmann until 1939.